TABLE OF CONTENTS

FOREWORD	i
PREFACE	iii
O Worship the Lord in the Beauty of Holiness – Why We Go To Church	1
Our Epiphany Challenge	10
Devotional Reading for Lent	12
The Meaningful Use of the Means of Grace as the Source of Spiritual Life	18
Liturgical Commonplaces	37
Luther's Theology of the Cross	52
The Sacrament an Easter Affair	58
How to Give Up the Confessions without Seeming To	64
The Lord's Supper	70
Unreal Language about the Real Presence	78
Turbulence and Division	81
What Does Baptism Mean For Daily Living?	89
Regular Prayer and the Ministry	96
Professor Marquart Discusses Liturgy from Confessional Viewpoint	99
Liturgy and Evangelism	101
Gold, Silver, and Bronze and Closed Communion	104
Lutheran Worship and the Golden Middle	107
Contemporary Services	110
INDEX	112

FOREWORD

Dr. Marquart was a beloved Professor by all the students that sat in his classes. His ability to simplify great theological concepts made him a favorite Teacher for all the students who attended the Seminary. He not only instilled in us a love for Theology, but he also showed us how it was to be applied in a pastor's daily calling.

However, these writings are not just for pastors. Even dedicated laymen will be able to grasp and learn from this great Teacher of the Church. Whenever and wherever Dr. Marquart made a presentation, you would soon see that he was eagerly sought out, not just by pastors but also by laymen. They too recognized his genius in refuting those who denied the Word of God. He was as popular with laymen as he was with pastors. Here in these volumes you will once again be able to take your place and listen to this great Teacher, as he clearly enunciates various topics from a thoroughly Lutheran perspective. Since these multiple volumes consist of the various topics that Dr. Marquart addressed over his illustrious life, you will find it hard to put these volumes down.

Having Dr. Marquart's writings in book form will once again allow this fearless Champion of the Church to speak to the issues that continue to plague the Church from one generation to the next. False doctrine continues to be rehashed and sent out with new clothes. As the Proverb goes, "there is nothing new under the sun." Dr. Marquart had the remarkable ability to dissect what the issue was, and why it was, and still is, false doctrine. Confessional Lutherans from all over the world were always eager to attend Dr. Marquart's lectures. They recognized that he was a giant among men. Anyone concerned about the welfare of the Church will want to have these volumes on their bookshelf.

It appears that the Almighty Savior of the Church, in His infinite wisdom, chooses to send out only a few Teachers of the Church. One may make a very short list of these esteemed gifts from God. Luther, Chemnitz, Gerhard, Walther, Pieper, Preus, and Marquart. Their writings stand the test of time. These men did not write for some passing fad, that is here today and then blown away by tomorrow's changing wind vane. Any pastor or layman, who has a desire and love for the Truth, will not be disappointed with these volumes. Every congregation that has a love for the Lord and His saving Gospel, would do well to purchase the writings from these Teachers of the Church. God had His good reasons for raising these men up and sending them out, and it would be wise for pastors and laymen to read, mark, learn and inwardly digest the writings of these great defenders of the Gospel.

Rev. Herman Otten is to be commended for publishing the writings of Dr. Kurt Marquart. This may well be Rev. Otten's finest and most enduring contribution to the Church.

Rev. Ray R. Ohlendorf
Salem Lutheran Church
Taylorsville, NC
4th Sunday in Lent 2014

Acknowledgements

Well Herman,

As usual you find yourself doing what unsere beliebte Synode should have done long ago. The fact that CPH has not already published a book of Kurt's writings is an absolute travesty. It is an indictment of the politics before theology which has destroyed the orthodoxy of the LCMS. Our Savior Lutheran Church will stand by you in the worthy project. Back in the dark days when Bohlmann and his supporters were after Robert Preus we published a number of Kurt's magnificent essays on Robert's behalf. Modern Missouri has never produced another theologian comparable to him either in confessional fidelity or eloquence. We are proud and eager to take part in this belated effort. "Gottes Wort Und Luthers Lehr Vergehet Nun Und Nimmermehr."

Larry White, Pastor
Our Saviour Lutheran Church
Houston, Texas

Thanks to Luke Otten for arranging the publication of these volumes and to Naomi Finck, Natalie Hoerstkamp, for type-setting.

Thanks to Grace Otten for recognizing the importance of publishing *Marquart's Works* ever since they first began appearing in *Christian News* more than 50 years ago. Thanks to Scott Meyer, "America's confessional Lutheran" lay historian and President of the Concordia Historical Institute whose appreciation of Marquart's works and encouragement helped make the publication of these volumes possible.

PREFACE

Dr. C. F. W. Walther, first president of The Lutheran Church-Missouri Synod, has been rightly referred to as "The American Luther." As the editor of a Christian weekly for 51 years, the undersigned has reviewed thousands of books. During all these years he has published the writings of many theologians. The index at the back of Volume V of the *Christian News Encyclopedia* lists the names of hundreds of theologians whose writings have appeared in *Christian News*. Some, like Kurt Marquart, were also good friends. Yet, the editor knows of no theologian who deserves the title "The International Lutheran" more than Kurt Marquart. The editor's wife, Grace, is a graduate of Concordia College, St. Paul Minnesota and Valparaiso University. There she studied under some prominent theologians who later became professors at Concordia Seminary, St. Louis and Seminex. In 1963 Grace Otten and Kurt Marquart were *CN*'s reporters at the Fourth Assembly of the Lutheran World Federation in Helsinki, Finland. Following the LWF Assembly she and the editor's brother, Walter, who knew Marquart for 54 years, accompanied him on a twenty city lecture tour in the U.S. Grace shares the editor's evaluation of Kurt Marquart. She helped make it possible together with Luke Otten, Ruth Rethemeyer, Mary Beth Otten, Kristina Bailey and the Missourian Publishing Company, Washington, Missouri, to get *Marquart's Legacy* published in 2006 not long after his death. The 76 page *Marquart's Legacy* is available from *Christian News* for $5.00. It includes photos of Marquart and family and information about two professionally made videos showing Marquart in action.

Marquart's Legacy begins with a brief biography of Kurt Marquart. Then follows "Remembrances of a Former Seminary Roommate," the editor of *Christian News*. Next comes "The Lasting Legacy of Kurt Marquart" as expressed by many who knew him well.

The appendixes list the writings and reports of Kurt Marquart which have appeared in 44 volumes of *Christian News* (1962-2006), *A Christian Handbook on Vital Issues*, the five volumes of the *Christian News Encyclopedia, Luther Today, What Would He Do or Say?* and *Crisis in Christendom-Seminex Ablaze*. The lasting legacy of a great theologian and genius like Kurt Marquart can best be found in his works. *CN* suggested in 2006 that the Lutheran Church-Missouri Synod's Concordia Publishing House should publish *Marquart's Works*.

The questions at the end of each section are included to make *Marquart's Works* helpful for study. In an age when faith in historic Christianity is declining in all of the major denominations, *Marquart's Works* can be used to encourage and strengthen faithful Christians and begin a 21st Century Reformation and 21st Century *Formula of Concord* by the 500th anniversary of the Reformation in 2017.

Herman Otten
Reformation, 2014

"O WORSHIP THE LORD IN THE BEAUTY OF HOLINESS"

April 6, 1964

Why We Go To Church

I

(Some Thoughts on Meaningful Worship)
Every Christian is a priest, 1 Peter 2: 5-9. The chief function of a priest is to worship Almighty God. The very First Commandment deals with worship. "And the Christian Faith is this", says the Athanasian Creed: "that we *worship* one God in Trinity, and Trinity in Unity". True religion is first and foremost not morality, ethics, or even doctrine (though these are essential), much less is it any sort of activism, but it is worship. And our Lutheran Confessions often remind us that the highest, best worship, most acceptable to God is faith itself, that is, penitence for sin, crucifixion of the flesh, longing for divine forgiveness, joyful, grateful acceptance of the Gospel promise, that is, firm trust in the most holy merit of Christ, our only Savior. This faith is the essence of spiritual life, and from it flow the fruits of the Spirit: love, joy, peace, longsuffering, gentleness, goodness, faith, meekness, temperance (self-control). Gal. 5:22-23. To create and sustain in us this faith and spiritual life, God has appointed external means, the Word and the Sacraments, that is, the Gospel in all its forms, written, spoken, sung, or signed. Around these means of grace the whole Christian life revolves.

It is evident that the first work of the Church, and therefore of each Christian congregation, is the corporate adoration of God in Christ. All other activities, such as missions, instruction in divine truth, charitable works, and so on, flow from and lead to worship. In fact, the whole Christian life is an act of worship. Unlike other Church activities, worship, in the specific sense, will continue throughout Eternity. In this connection, consult the following texts of Holy Scripture: Ps. 84:1-4 St. Luke 2: 36-38; Ephesians 2: 19-22; Colossians 3:1-2-16; Philippians 2:10-11; Hebrews 10:21-25; 12:22-24; 13: 10-15; Rev. 7: 15.

One Great Meaningful Unit

The main public order of worship of the Christian, Church, about which all minor services and devotions, public and private, revolve, is the divine Liturgy, the Service of Word and Sacrament. This historical Liturgy is one great meaningful unit, an organic whole. It is not the creation of any one individual and his whim, but it is the possession of the whole Church. Nor does it at all resemble the camel, which is said by some to be the animal which "looks as if it had been put together by a committee"! Much less is the Liturgy any sort of dead, musty, antiquarian curiosity. The Liturgy is rather the living, growing tissue of the Church's Spirit-filled devotion. Have you ever noticed that the Liturgy consists almost completely of Scriptural sentences and phrases? It is God-centered, not man-centered. That is why the Liturgy is deeply beautiful and religiously, spiritually satisfying, never superficially "pretty" and theatrically, psychologically "effective", in the cheap, calculated sense of many a modern Protestant "worship program". And the elevated, majestic brevity, simplicity, and restraint of its language have been shaped by the living, praying faith of many generations, yes, of millions of Christians throughout the world, the way pebbles are smoothed and rounded by centuries of waves and wavelets in the churning seas.

Our Liturgy Must "Make Sense"
It is particularly important in our day of worldliness, of pre-occupation with activities and organizations, in the midst of spiritual coldness and indifference, to have a proper perspective in this matter; for large sections of Christendom seem to have drawn the conclusion, for all practical purposes, that since Christianity is the religion of the Word, therefore it is a religion of words, or talk! (Revivalism especially breeds a nauseating, compulsive religious chatter, mistaken for spirituality). There are those who think of religion as a matter of instilling proper knowledge in people's heads. The conclusion is then drawn—whether this is clearly thought out or not—that one goes to church to hear sermons, and that nothing else in the Service really matters too much. All the rest is regarded as sort of a decorative setting, or window dressing, for the sermon! The next step would be to think that one might just as well stay home and listen to a sermon on the wireless. And it is indeed possible that the sermon we hear on the wireless on a given Sunday is more interesting, perhaps even more inspiring, than the one we hear in our own parish church. If hearing sermons were the only point, this would finish church-attendance! Such views, of course, do not favor our Synod.

The present explanation of the Liturgy will follow the Common Service (*Australian Lutheran Hymnbook,* p. 9), which represents essentially the historic Liturgy of the Western Church, and which is the normal rite used by the Lutheran Church throughout the English-speaking world. **This whole matter, incidentally is to come before the development of the real devotional life.** If we are to avoid stunted, spiritually shrivelled views of the Church, and if our participation in her public worship is to be meaningful, the Liturgy we celebrate on Sundays must really "make sense" to us. Otherwise we have only formalism. But with meaningful participation, the Liturgy can and should be a real spiritual adventure, a thrilling experience, a bit of Heaven on earth.

"That Spiritual Pilgrimage"
The structure of the Liturgy has been compared to that of a church-building. As the church consists of two main parts, the nave, where the people sit, and the chancel, where the Altar stands, plus a small entrance area or vestibule, called "narthex", so the Christian Liturgy consists of

two main parts, the Service of the Word and the Service of the Sacrament, preceded by a brief act of spiritual purification consisting of the Confession and Absolution.

We enter upon that spiritual pilgrimage which is the Liturgy with the Invocation: "In the Name of the Father, and of the Son, and of the Holy Ghost". This Invocation, spoken by the celebrating minister (the "celebrant"), and traditionally accompanied by the sign of the holy Cross (see your Catechism, p. 22) is a plea to the Most Holy Trinity, to Whose honor and glory every Liturgy is celebrated, to be present with His blessing, and graciously to receive our worship. The Invocation reminds us of the beginning of our spiritual life, in Holy Baptism, when we became children of the Triune Majesty, and received the sign of the holy Cross in token that we had been redeemed by Christ the Crucified, and henceforth belonged entirely to Him.

Kneeling in humble penitence, we confess our sins and pray God to cleanse us from them by his grace, for Christ's sake. We then receive the Absolution, which, spoken in accordance with St. John 20:21, removes from our souls the burden of guilt and its defilement. Thus absolved and cleansed, we are ready to approach the Divine Presence more closely.

II

The first main part of the Liturgy, the Service of the Word, now opens with the *Introit* (Latin for "entrance"), which is usually chanted by the choir, while the celebrant enters the chancel and goes up to the Altar. At one time a whole Psalm, even several Psalms, were chanted at this point. Now the Introit usually consists of an Antiphon (taken from the Psalter or from another portion of Holy Writ) a verse from a Psalm, and the *Gloria Patri* (Glory be to the Father and to the Son and to the Holy Ghost . . .). The Introit is to the Liturgy what an overture is to an opera: It gives the themes, and sets the mood for what is to follow. For no two Sundays in the Church Year have exactly the same Liturgy: During the first half of the Church Year, from Advent to Trinity Sunday, we follow, step by step, the earthly life of our divine Redeemer. All the great Feasts, such as Christmas, Epiphany, Easter, Ascension, and Pentecost, fall into this half of the year. The second half is the season of up to twenty-seven Sundays after Trinity, in which we consider the various gifts of grace with which Christ sanctifies His Church. Thus no aspect of Christian truth is left untouched by the liturgical cycle of the Christian Year. The parts of the Liturgy which change from Sunday to Sunday are called the "propers" (Introit, Collect, Epistle, Gradual, Gospel), while the standard part is called the "ordinary" of the Service. These changes from Sunday to Sunday, and from season to season, within the Liturgy, provide within a solid framework a rich and challenging rhythm for a healthy, balanced spiritual life and devotion!

In the *Kyrie* ("Lord, have mercy upon us . . .") we acknowledge God as our King, on Whom we depend for every blessing of body and soul. In this brief and sublime prayer, we beseech Him to supply all our needs, spiritual and temporal. We pray for ourselves, for each other, and for the whole Church of Christ on earth, in fact, for all mankind.

Christmas Every Sunday

God *has* supplied all our needs in the Gift of Himself! Therefore the pastor now intones the joyful *Gloria in Excelsis,* and the people continue: "and on earth peace, goodwill toward men. We praise Thee, we bless Thee, we worship Thee . . ." The opening portion of this solemn chant is that angelic Christmas hymn which was first heard by the shepherds of Bethlehem. But why a Christmas hymn at this point? Well, because each Liturgy is really, in a very profound sense, a repetition of Christmas. What is Christmas? The coming of Christ to His people! And that is exactly what happens in Word and Sacrament, culminating in the mystery of the Real Presence. It is very important to realize that the Liturgy is not merely a remembrance of something past, as a Christmas pageant would be, for example, but it is a celebration of a real, gracious coming of Christ, through Word and Sacrament, in the present, *here and now!*

While pastor and people were addressing God, the pastor faced the Altar. These portions of the Liturgy are called "sacrificial". The parts in which the celebrant speaks to the people on God's behalf, are called "sacramental", and this is symbolized by facing the people, for example in the Salutation, in which the pastor wishes the people the Presence of God: "The Lord be with you". They, in turn, respond: "And with thy spirit," meaning: May God sustain your spirit, so that you may please God in this public celebration of Word and Sacrament.

The Collect is the brief prayer for that day, in which we thank and praise God, and also ask Him for the particular blessing which we celebrate on that day. So, for example, we pray on Pentecost: "O God, Who didst teach the hearts of Thy faithful people by sending to them the light of Thy Holy Spirit, grant us by the same Spirit to have a right judgment in all things and evermore to rejoice in His holy comfort."

In the Epistle (meaning "letter", referring to the letters of the Apostles) Christ, instructs us through the Apostolic Word. After the *Gradual,* which connects Epistle and Gospel, and is sung by the choir, the Holy Gospel for the Day is read. This is the high point of this first part of the Service: Christ Himself is speaking His Life-giving words to us, through the inspired record of the Evangelist. We stand with devout attention. We express our joy in the Gospel by singing "Glory be to Thee O Lord!" before the reading, and "Praise be to Thee, O Christ", after it.

We Declare Our Faith

Having heard the Word of God, we declare our faith and our obedience in the Creed. The Creed appropriate here is the Nicene, adopted by the Council of Nicea in 325 A.D. The Apostles' Creed is the baptismal Creed, and is used at minor services, and frequently in private devotions. The Sermon then applies God's Word to us today. The important thing about the Sermon is not whether it pleases us, and so on, but whether it is God's Word. No man has the right to proclaim anything else from a Christian pulpit. His own notions and opinions do not belong there. For in the Sermon Christ Himself, in His Prophetic Office, speaks to each person present: "He that heareth you, heareth Me . . ." (St. Luke 10:16). It is an art to listen to sermons properly. The art consists in humbly applying the Sermon to *ourselves.* That means letting our hearts be crushed by the divine Law, so that we repent of our sins, are ashamed of the lukewarmness of our love, and are then comforted and strengthened by the Gospel, in which also we receive strength to love God and our neighbor more and more. The sermon, therefore, is not merely something interesting to engage the mind, much less is it a "performance", to be critically judged— we are of course to judge the doctrine expressed, and see whether it is Scriptural— but it is a divine claim upon our whole personality, body and soul, mind, will, and feelings!

Dr. Martin Luther writes:
"On the last day God will say to me: Have you preached that? And I will answer, Yes, exactly. Then God will turn to you and say, Have you also heard that? And you will answer, Yes. Then He will say further: Why, then, didn't you believe it? And you will say, O, I regarded it merely as the word of a man, since a poor chaplain or town pastor spoke it. Thus shall the same word which sticks to your heart accuse you and be your judge on the last day. For it is God's Word, it is God Himself whom you have heard, as Christ says, 'He that heareth you heareth Me.' I have sufficiently done my office before the tribunal and presence of God, for I have exposed your sins and offences and reprimanded you for them, and I pure of your blood. Now see how you stand." (WA 47: 120.)

In response to the whole first half of the Service, which is now drawing to a close, we sing the "Create in me" (Ps. 51), asking God to transform our hearts and lives by His Word, which we have heard, to make us good, fruitful soil, not the stony, hardened, or thorny kind, which loses or abuses the precious Seed.

Needs of the Church Needs of the World

A very important part of the Liturgy is the General Prayer, which follows now. In this prayer we bring before God the needs of the whole Church and of the whole world, asking Him, for the sake of the most holy merit of Christ, to bestow such blessings as all mankind need for their spiritual and temporal welfare. Since the Church is God's Family on earth, each member is concerned about the needs of all other members. Thus special prayers of intercession are added for particular people in our parish, in their joys, sorrows, afflictions, and trials. Do not hesitate, therefore, to ask your pastor for such special prayers at important times in life, for example when there is a serious illness in your family, if someone is about to have an operation, or if there is joy and thanksgiving over a new baby!

It is also a good custom to present the offerings to God during the General Prayer, with such words as: "Receive, O God, our bodies and souls, our hearts and minds, our talents and powers, together with the offerings we bring before Thee, for Thou hast purchased us to be Thine own." It is clear then that in the offering we have to do not with a mere "collection", but with a holy sacrifice, an act of adoration, in which our gifts upon the Altar represent that "living sacrifice" of our total selves which is our "reasonable service", Romans 12:1. We either offer ourselves to God completely, or we do not offer ourselves at all. He does not want merely a part of us. And our offering must express this fact. How wrong and sacrilegious, therefore, carelessly to toss in a few coins, leftovers, out of habit, or because it is expected of us! That is not a pleasing sacrifice, but an abomination in the sight of God. It amounts to throwing a tip in God's direction, and expecting Him to be grateful for the insult!

It is better not to put anything at all into the offering basket, than to put in something which is not a real sacrifice of our substance and of our love, in short, a real token of self-surrender.

III

The Service of the Sacrament

In the ancient Church people used to bring food and other things, which were later distributed to the poor. Some of the bread and wine would be taken and placed on the Altar for the Holy Communion. The human gifts of bread and wine became the earthly bearers of the divine. Gift of the body and blood of Christ! St. Augustine the great Church Father, once, having selected the bread and wine from among the gifts, pointed at the chalice, and said to his congregation: "You are in that chalice!" He meant that our offerings merely represent ourselves. Compare, therefore, your sacrifice for God with what you spend for your own pleasure. Our giving is a good index of our love for God. When giving, therefore, do not think merely of a congregational budget (such things as salaries, or even painting, plumbing, and the like), nor of your so-called "fair share", etc., but think of God Himself, and His benefits and gifts to us. It is to Him that we give through His Church. And remember that God's needs are great, because, though He needs nothing in Himself, He has graciously chosen to make the needs of men His own: "...ye have done it unto Me!" (St. Matthew 25:40).

But no matter how much we give to God, it is nothing compared to the Gift for which we now prepare our souls in the Communion Preface, which opens the second half of the divine Liturgy, the Service of the Sacrament. We are ready to enter into the Holy of Holies of the New Testament. We lift up our hearts and give thanks unto the Lord our God, in words and music, which come from the earliest ages of the Faith, when the blood of the martyrs, which is the seed of the Church, flowed freely. Our word "Eucharist", by the way, comes from the Greek word for thanksgiving. It shows that the Communion is a joyful, happy occasion, not a sad and funereal one! Then we unite with angels and archangels, with the whole Church in Heaven and on earth, as we adore the Triune Majesty in the solemn *Sanctus* ("Holy, holy, holy . . ."), the scraphic hymn of adoration revealed to the prophet Isaiah (Chapter Six) in a vision. To this sacred chant are added the words from the Psalter: "Blessed is He that cometh in the name of the Lord. Hosanna in the highest!" With this exclamation, amid glad Hosannas, the people of Jerusalem welcomed Christ, their King, on the first Palm Sunday. The Church today uses the same words in welcoming her King, Who is about to come, this time not on a humble donkey, but in equally humble bread and wine.

The Prayer of Our Lord, the Our Father, is now chanted. This, the greatest of all prayers, is fittingly the Table Prayer of the Christian Church, at the Table of her Lord! That Table is now prepared as the celebrant chants the Consecration, which consists of the Words of Institution, recorded in Holy Scripture. Before coming to the Altar, the Congregation chants the *Agnus Dei* ("O Christ, Thou Lamb of God, that takest away the sin of the world, have mercy upon us, and grant us Thy peace!")

"God's Own Sacrifice Complete"

Then we kneel at the Altar, and receive the true body and blood of God, that same body and blood which were sacrificed for our redemption, by which God Himself rendered to himself a perfect satisfaction and reparation for all sins of all men of all times and places. Through this wonderful Gift, the perfect Sacrifice of Christ on Calvary, "God's own Sacrifice complete", is applied to us personally, individually. God cleanses us from the guilt and power of sin, strengthens our faith and love, gives us His own divine and eternal Life, and above all, gives us Himself in true and blessed Communion. It is a foretaste of the Heavenly Banquet, at which, in Eternity, we shall be the privileged guests of the lamb of God.

After the Communion we praise God in the words of the aged Simeon, who, when he had held in His arms the blessed Christ-Child, his Savior, exclaimed: "Lord, now lettest Thou Thy servant depart in peace, for mine eyes have seen Thy Salvation . . ." Our eyes too have seen our Salvation, and having received the same holy Body which Simeon once held, we depart in peace. A brief prayer of thanks is followed by the Benediction, in which God, through His appointed servant, gives us His blessing. Having touched God, and having been nourished and strengthened in spirit by Him, we go forth with His blessing, to our homes, our work, our daily life, with renewed energy, and with transforming joy, faith, and love.

It is clear from the above that the Liturgy is a meaningful whole, a unit, an organism. Just as a play by Shakespeare makes complete sense only when the last act is added, no matter how good the first are in themselves, so the Liturgy, historically and theologically, is a meaningful unit including both Word and Sacrament. The Apostolic Church celebrated both Word and Sacrament at least every Sunday. In Acts 20:7 we read: "And upon the first day of the week, when the disciples came together to break bread . . ." And Article 24 of both the Augsburg Confession and the

Apology, asserts that our churches celebrate the complete Service, including the Sacrament, every Sunday and holy day. Some sixteenth and seventeenth century Lutheran church orders even provided that if there were no communicants on a given Sunday, so that the Sacrament could not be celebrated, an admonition against despising the Sacrament was to be read!

Beware of Losing Balance

In losing the liturgical outlook, much of modern Protestantism has lost far more than dignity and beauty: it has lost its balance, its basic religious sense and orientation, its meaning! Consider the lament of a modernistic journal:

> For what important tasks does this essential institution (the Church) demand its members' loyalty? Church suppers where macaroni casseroles provide a prelude to a travelogue about the South Sea Islands? Card parties where women pass an afternoon in the verbal slaughter of their friends, pay 200 dollars for the privilege and earn 10.13 dollars for the church? Couples Clubs where crowds of gracious people gather for a Christmas dance and go away convinced that the town does not need a country club after all since the church takes care of their needs so nicely? Attendance records where the contribution of the soul is less important than the presence of the body? *(The Pulpit,* July, 1960).

Many thinking people realize that much of modern church-life is an undignified farce. Of course Protestantism's troubles are not merely liturgical. The doctrinal decay is the real malady. And that cannot be cured with liturgical disguises, as some are trying to do. But that is not the Liturgy; that is empty ritualism, formalism.

Divine revelation is the very heart and core of the Liturgy. Without this doctrinal base, it is but a feeble, empty parody! The same forces that attack the Liturgy, also attack divine doctrine. The attitude which refuses to bend the knee in humble adoration before Jehovah in the burning bush, is the same attitude which approaches the bush with scientific instruments to measure the heat and analyze its nature! Liturgy and Dogma belong inseparably together! Without Dogma, "Liturgy" is a putrid, poisonous jungle, and without Liturgy, that is, devotion, "Dogma" becomes distorted into an arid desert of intellectualism.

It is clear, then, that the Liturgy, properly understood and practiced, is far more than a mere decorative setting for the sermon! It is not a little ceremony to be "got over with", or some sort of performance to be watched passively: It is rather a divine-human drama, in which we, the priests of God, actively participate. It is something that requires our wholehearted, enthusiastic participation and involvement, in body and soul! The more we learn to "let ourselves go" spiritually, and really throw ourselves into the grandeur of the Liturgy, in word and act, so that these become the expressions of our own devotion, the more we will learn to value this Sunday experience as the center of our lives, and the secret of our strength, to which, as to a Mount of Transfiguration, a Paradise, we gladly and longingly ascend week after week; for in this Service of Word and Sacrament God in His infinite goodness allows His Heaven to touch, heal, and bless our sin-sick, cold, barren earth!

Lutheran News, April 6, 1964, July 15, 1964, August 10, 1964

1. Every Christian is a ____ whose chief function is to ____.
2. True religion is first and foremost ____.
3. The whole Christian life is an act of ____.
4. The historical Liturgy is one ____.
5. The Liturgy is not the creation of ____.
6. Why does the Liturgy not resemble a camel? ____
7. The Liturgy consists almost completely of ____.
8. How was the Liturgy shaped? ____
9. Revivalism breeds a ____.
10. The Liturgy must really make ____ to us, otherwise we have ____.
11. The liturgy should be a bit of ____ on ____.
12. Introit is Latin for ____.
13. What are the "propers"? ____
14. Each Liturgy is a repetition of ____.
15. What is the difference between the "sacrificial" and "sacramental" parts of the Liturgy? ____
16. The importance about the sermon is ____
17. What is the art of listening to a sermon? ____
18. Do not hesitate to ask your pastor for ____.
19. In the offering we do not have to do with a mere ____ but with ____.
20. What is not a pleasing sacrifice? ____
21. Our giving is a good index of ____.
22. Why are God's needs great? ____
23. "Eucharist" comes from the Greek word meaning ____.
24. What is the Angus Dei? ____
25. The Liturgy is a meaningful ____.
26. In losing the liturgical outlook much of modern Protestantism has lost ____.
27. Thinking people realize that much of modern church life is ____.
28. The real malady of Protestantism's troubles is ____.
29. Without Dogma, "Liturgy" is ____ and without Liturgy, "Dogma" becomes ____.

OUR EPIPHANY CHALLENGE

January 11, 1965

Epiphany! Christmas of the Gentiles, when the very learned Wise Men join the very simple shepherds in adoring the Divine Baby! And in answer to God's great Gift, they bring the first known human Christmas gifts.

We who have knelt at the Manger of the Savior and rejoiced at His holy Birth, have the sacred privilege of making this Child known and loved as far as the influence of our lives extends. Even one little star, shining brightly for Christ, makes a tremendous difference to the Kingdom of God . . . And every Christian is called to be such a star!

In this new year of Our Lord, 1965, our missionary task has particular urgency. As usual, there are two forces arrayed against the Church: the unbelief of a pagan, decaying world from without, and the unbelief of heresy, of apostasy, from within. But both forces are unusually pointed today: A large part of the world is ruled by tyrants, who aim to enslave the world and are doggedly—and, so far, successfully!—working toward that goal. As for the Church, we are faced with two significant developments:

(1) Rome and the "Ecumenical Movement" (World Council of Churches, Lutheran World Federation, etc.), representing different anti-Christian tendencies, are moving toward each other. The Vatican seems to be making every effort to make itself more attractive to "modern man" and, given a few decades, perhaps a century or two, may well succeed in absorbing most of Eastern Orthodoxy and Protestantism into one great and glittering Babylonian Captivity!

(2) The world-wide fellowship of Confessional Lutheran Churches is beginning to show signs of breaking up. The Missouri Synod in North America, for a century the foremost champion of the pure Word and Sacraments, has lately shown itself to be a leaking vessel, with the waters of the modern "theology" of doubt rushing in so fast that only a dramatic, miraculous reversal can save the sinking ship. Should Missouri go down—and this seems imminent—great confusion will result elsewhere. Already the North American Synodical Conference has broken up. A complete re-alignment of the Confessional Lutheran forces of the world seems to be developing.

Solely Needed in These Troubled Times Is An Informed Laity!

The seriousness of the situation can hardly be overestimated. Our generation seems destined to live through some great and historic upheavals in Church and State.

Nevertheless we face the future calmly and without fear. If demonic Communism comes, and martyrdom be our fate, then so be it. We pray only for faith and strength. And if the storms of doctrinal confusion should seem for a time to shatter the True Visible Church on earth into fragments, then we shall grieve, but we shall not despair, for we know that the Church is founded upon the Rock and that the very gates of hell shall not prevail against her. After the storm, if the world stands, God will again send peace and unity, when, where, and how He pleases.

This is not a time for fair-weather Christians. It is a time for soul-searching, for penitence, for truth, a time for prayer, for devotion, for sacrifice. If Christ be our Anchor, then come what may: we shall not be moved!

In the remaining time of grace—be it long or short—let us eagerly encourage each other in spiritual life, in faith and love, that we, our families, and our congregations, may cling to Christ where He manifests Himself: in His Word and Sacraments. And let us manifest Him to the desperate, dying world around us, by visibly living the Kingdom of God on earth, living it with a convincing urgency and a consuming love. And our King and Father will bless us with every good gift from above, and will grant us the final victory!

K. E. Marquart

Lutheran News, January 11, 1965

1. Every Christian is called to be ____.
2. What are two forces arrayed against the Church? ____
3. Rome and the ecumenical movement are ____.
4. The Missouri Synod has shown itself to be ____.
5. What seems imminent? ____

DEVOTIONAL READING FOR LENT

Review Article

February 8, 1965

"Communion with Christ" is the title of an attractive new paperback by W. J. Fields, recently published by C.P.H.

The days are long past, unfortunately, when the mere Concordia label sufficed to guarantee the orthodoxy of a book. But the present little volume is very admirable in many ways. The able, lucid exposition—equally free of the safe triteness's of popular "devotional" literature, and of the contorted affectations (pseudo-nouns like "once-for-all-ness") which give an illiterate, grunting effect to "chic" popularizations—makes the book an ideal gift for Confirmands, young or old. It is bound to deepen the reader's sacramental understanding and devotion.

Some will undoubtedly feel that the book is a product of the "high church" Liturgical Movement, and as such suspect.

No Romanizing Interpretations

But this is too simple. It is true that the Liturgical Movement within American Lutheranism is often more Anglican and Romanizing than Lutheran. Lutheran theology simply does not allow the sacerdotalist concepts of Church, Ministry, and Ordination, the anti-sermon sacramentalism (including reservation of the elements), and other peculiarities of a decidedly Pelagian flavor, which characterize the official Liturgical Movement. (An Interesting feature, possibly imported via later Anglican Ritualism, is the liaison with Liberalism in an anti-dogmatic mysticism!) When the Lutheran Confessions are quoted in support of such notions, as they often are, they are being misconstrued. Perhaps some writers consciously imitate Newman's Tract XC treatment of the Anglican 39 Articles. If so, a great distortion is being perpetrated. For while the Anglican Articles are indeed vague, inclusivism, latitudinarian, and this by intention, the Lutheran Confessions are doctrinally precise and explicit and definitely do not allow of waxen nose Romanizing "interpretations"!

It is, however, also true that heretical movements usually start out with a legitimate concern or grievance, which is then distorted through over-emphasis. The Liturgical Movement is no exception. Much as one must deplore the silly infatuation with Roman or Eastern Orthodox ceremonial which seems to be bred by the Movement, one must, if one is fair, admit that these excesses have been provoked by other excesses in the opposite direction. The rich devotional heritage of the Lutheran Church has been allowed to fall into disrepair, and to be replaced by Reformed pietism, theatricality, and anti-sacramentalism. If now the child is clawing at walls and eating dirt, one may have to admit a deficiency in his diet.

F. Lochner, Dr. Walther's coworker, clearly foresaw the danger, and warned against it:

"Nevertheless various observations cause not only me but others also to fear that which has, as a fruit of the pure doctrine, been granted us now also in the Liturgy, will gradually again be exchanged, in later times, for the bare puritanical manner, which was once dominant here..." (*Lehre U. Wehre*, vol. 8, quoted in *Hauptgottesdienst*, p. V).

A Horrified Report

So bare and puritanical had the older, Eastern Lutheranism become by the middle of the last century, that the practice of the Confessional synods or the mid-west seemed disgustingly Roman Catholic by comparison. The *Lutheraner* for Sept. 23, 1856, gleefully reprints, under the heading "Peter in der Fremde" (Peter in a Foreign Country), the reactions of an Eastern Lutheran, J. B. McAfee, to Pastor Schaller's Service in St. Louis. Mr. McAfee had written a horrified report for the *Lutheran Observer* from which the Missouri publication quotes:

"Here I saw, for the first time in a Lutheran Church, images and a Crucifix. I came to the conclusion that I had come to the wrong place and was in a Roman church. The preacher was dressed in priestly vestments (Priesterkleidung). The Sacrament was to be celebrated. Wax-candles were burning on the east side of the Altar, wafers were used, etc. People bowed toward the images, and, as I supposed, before them. (Here the editor inserted the following correction: 'That is untrue. We bow before no images, but we begin the Altar Service by bowing, with a quiet sigh to God. D.L.'). Thus the ceremony ended. I have rarely seen a preacher ostensibly more solemn, earnest, and zealous. But don't think that, because I admire the zeal of the man (Brother Schaller), I admire the ceremony. That is something to which I am utterly opposed."

Pastor Fields is probably aware that the old Lutheran attitude and practice in respect to the Sacrament of the Altar would be similarly foreign to many contemporary Lutherans. And he was very wise in avoiding extravagant controversial formulations which would have destroyed the value of the book. The extremist, anti-evangelical Romanizing flavor of the Liturgical Movement is delightfully absent. Luther, and the usual Confessional excerpts (Augsburg Confession XXIV) are cited.

Anti-Sacramental Practice

Pastor Fields wishes to lead Lutherans deeper into their own Lutheran, Scriptural appreciation of the Holy Communion. He understands the mentality that has developed in the past two centuries, and which exhibits, frequently, the paradox of a tenacious adherence to the dogmatic, polemical definitions concerning the Real Presence on the one hand, combined with an apparent non-valuation of the Sacrament in Church life and personal piety on the other. Too often Sacramental theory is combined with what amounts to anti-Sacramental practice. The author meets this mentality relevantly and tactfully:

"You do, or course, receive forgiveness of sins in the written and spoken Gospel, and in that sense the sacrament is not an absolute necessity. But you can live, too, if you have only one lung. You can exist with only one kidney... Christians therefore do not ask whether they must partake of the sacrament, any more than they ask whether they must worship God. They rather thank God for all the means that He has established whereby He imparts His forgiving grace to His church and to their lives" (p. 42).

"As you receive your Savior's life into your own, ask that what He was may become also a part of you; that you be concerned more with loving than with being loved, with serving than with being served, with helping than with being helped, with understanding than with being understood" (p. 53).

"Paul says that one of the reasons why there were many who were 'weak and sickly' among the Corinthians (I Cor. 11:30) was the lack of a full and proper use of the sacrament. Perhaps he could have been referring to congregations as well as to individuals when he said this ... if the sacrament is placed at the center of the corporate life of the parish, rather than on the periphery, and if the Christians in the parish enjoy a rich understanding of the full power of the sacrament, partaking of it frequently and regularly, thinking of their parish as well as their personal problems, then that parish will be one where Christians grow in an understanding of their real purpose as a parish..." (p. 79).

"If one had to wait until he were 'worthy' then the church would have to eliminate the celebration of the sacrament because no one would ever be able to partake... Being a Christian never depends upon how we feel; it depends entirely upon what Christ has done for us... It should be noted that Scripture does not speak of 'unworthy communicants,' but rather of 'unworthy participation.' There is a difference. The Christian's concern should not be whether or not he is 'worthy' to receive the sacrament. He never is. His concern should rather be that he receive the sacrament in a worthy fashion" (pp. 86-90).

"Every hungry boy knows that when mother calls, 'Dinner is ready,' she is not issuing a command, but rather a most pleasant invitation" (p. 93).

"There are those who are afraid of the routine and mechanical in the frequent celebration of the sacrament ... The answer for this lies, of course, in a continual honest self-examination of our lives under the Law of God ... The more one understands his need of God's mercy, the less the pouring of that mercy into his life will become a matter of mere rote" (p. 94).

The congregation that offers the sacrament often is not limiting its members in the exercise of their faith. Those who feel no weekly (or more frequent) need for the sacrament are not obligated to partake that often. Those, on the other hand, whose hunger yearns for a more frequent participation, have opportunity to satisfy that hunger. The congregation that celebrates the sacrament infrequently limits its membership in the exercise of their faith. Those who desire and feel a need for more frequent communing are denied it.

"We might add that the weekly celebration of the sacrament is good Lutheran practice" (p. 96).

Acid-Baths of Liberalism

A disappointing feature of the book is the fact that "authorities" like Dietrich Bonhoeffer and the *Cresset* are cited. This will not endear the treatise to those Lutherans who understand what is happening to their beloved Church, and who are forced to watch, painfully helpless, as their leaders—unable or unwilling to comprehend—become possessed by ever more grandiose schemes for "sharing" the Faith—by dipping it into the acid baths of Liberalism!

The author could have found better, more solid ammunition in orthodox sources, such as the incomparable works of a Chemnitz, a Gerhard, or a Scriver. The Chemnitz-Leyser-Gerhard *Evangelical Harmony* has many wonderfully instructive, inspiring, and quotable references to the Eucharist. Or take Dr. Walther's monumental edition of Baier's *Compendium of Theology* (St. Louis, 1879). One little note on p. 529 of Vol. III beautifully anticipates modern "Biblical insights" into the nature of New Testament worship: The Holy Supper is described as the "nervus et vinculum congressuum ecclesiasticorum, I Cor. 11, 20" (strength and bond of the ecclesiastical assemblies). Gerhard is quoted regarding one of the "less principal purposes" of Holy Communion: "That we might preserve the public assemblies of the Christians, the strength and bond (nervus et vinculum) of which is the celebration of the Holy Supper, I Cor. 11,20."

And then there is F. Lochner, Dr. Walther's colleague, who, writing in *Lehre and Wehre* as well as in his *Hauptgottesdienst*, informs that many 16th century Lutheran liturgies (e.g. those of Pomerania, 1563, Liegnitz, 1594, Wittenberg 1559-1565, Mecklenburg, 1540-1552) provided that if on a given Sunday the Sacrament could not be celebrated for lack of communicants, a set or extemporaneous admonition should be given, "in which, without legalistic pressuring, the lack of communicants was deplored, and people were admonished and encouraged toward frequent reception of the most venerable Supper."

The Jungkuntz-Gehrke Pamphlet

Strange to say, some modern works which seek to restore the early Lutheran sacramental attitudes, are weak on the very point of the Real Presence! Reed's *Lutheran Liturgy* for example, nowhere clearly confesses the Real Presence but contains some very suspicious formulations which criticize the old, uncompromising dogmatic definitions. And the Jungkuntz-Gehrke pamphlet *Our Way Of Worship* contains the disturbing assertion that as regards Word and Sacrament, Christ is "as really present through the one as through the other." Of course, Christ is really present through the Word, but the Real Presence of His body and blood in the Sacrament is different, unique and without parallel in the other means of grace. Fields, on the other hand deals with the Real Presence clearly and unambiguously. He definitely confesses the Scriptural doctrine against the spiritualizing view (p. 22 Cf.). His statement that "many churches in the Reformed tradition" hold that what is eaten and drunk is "still nothing more than bread and wine," should read more correctly "all churches;" for even the Anglican Church—despite individual exceptions in this crazy-quilt body—is officially committed, in the 39 Articles, to a rejection of the Real Presence.

Apostolic Doctrine

Perhaps the weakest chapter, not *for* what it says, but for what it fails to say, is the one entitled "Communion and Fellowship."

Pastor Fields is quite right of course in stressing the New Testament fellowship over against the modern church-as-club notions. And he rightly emphasizes the corporate aspects of the sacrament, and its primary relation to the Universal Church, rather than to an outward organization. But this is not enough. Apostolic doctrine is the first, fundamental, and constitutive factor in the "unit concept" of Acts 2:42: "And they continued steadfastly in the apostles' doctrine and fellowship and in breaking of bread and in prayers." To loosen the connection in any way, and to practice this fellowship, breaking of bread, and prayers where adherence to the Apostles' doctrine is no more than a formality, if it is even that, would be contrary to the Second Commandment.

The author states that ordinarily only Lutherans will be admitted to Lutheran altars. But then this is qualified: "All Christians who commit their lives to Him and who understand the sacramental presence of the blessed Christ in the sacrament will want to receive it, and should not be denied it" (p. 80).

Very well, but can Christians really be said to "commit their lives to Him," to "understand the sacramental presence" or to give "whole-souled commitment to the Christ" if they either refuse steadfastly to submit to any part of the Apostles' doctrine, or excuse themselves from facing the issue by declaring the matter unimportant and minor? Can a sincere Christian, upon proper instruction, really "understand the sacramental presence" and nevertheless insist on continuing in a church-body which rejects this presence?

There is the tendency nowadays, to sweep such dogmatic difficulties under the rug. But they won't stay there. They insist on being faced and dealt with. Perhaps Pastor Fields will deal more fully and more adequately with this highly important, basic issue in a future edition. The confessing body, the True Visible Church, must never be seen merely as an "organization," but should be seen as the concrete local, legitimate embodiment of the Universal Church, recognized by the Marks, the pure Word and Sacraments, alone. To wish to deal with the one Church on any other basis—such as one's personal conjectures of who might not be a Christian—is Church-destroying enthusiasm. Since this unionistic fever is the great spiritual malady of our times, Christians need to be thoroughly grounded, again and again, especially also in connection with the Holy Sacrament, in the true objective, Apostolic doctrine of the Church!

Communion With Christ will make excellent and most rewarding devotional reading for Lent, in preparation for the Maundy Thursday Communion.

Christian News, February 8, 1965

1. Lutheran theology does not allow the sacerdotalist concepts of ____.
2. The Lutheran Confessions do not allow the ____.
3. Being a Christian never depends on how we ____.
4. A weekly celebration of the sacrament is good____.
5. A disappointing feature of "Communion With Christ" is ____.
6. Reed's Lutheran Liturgy nowhere confesses ____.
7. The 39 Articles of the Anglican Church rejects ____.
8. "This ____ fervor is the great spiritual malady of our times."

THE MEANINGFUL USE OF THE MEANS OF GRACE AS THE SOURCE OF SPIRITUAL LIFE

June 27, 1966, July 11, 1966, August 8, 1966

I. From the General to the Particular

At a time when it is popularly believed that the divisions and differences among Christian churches are about customs, forms of worship, organization, and details of "interpretation," it is very necessary to stress again and again that the decisive differences are about doctrine. Since the Gospel is THE Means of Grace, and since doctrinal differences really mean disagreements about the meaning of the Gospel, it is not surprising to find that all important doctrinal conflicts show up clearly in the doctrine of the Means of Grace. Here the Lutheran Church lives between two fronts; Rome on the one side and Geneva on the other. The one subverts the Means by falsifying Grace, the other sabotages Grace by short-circuiting the Means! Only as she maintains this double front, defending the Word against Rome, and the Sacraments against Geneva, does the Lutheran Church have the right to exist—or even the ability to survive!

But among all the tremendous mysteries of our Faith, is not the doctrine of the Means of Grace a rather minor, subsidiary point, and the disagreements more academic than real?

Let us take an example from physics. Electricity is a tremendous power. Rightly controlled, it can save, prolong, and ease human life, and vastly extend man's power over his environment. Out of control, it can kill, maim, and destroy. Now, the nature and properties of electricity make a fascinating subject for study; but no amount of knowledge or theory can take the place of an ordinary power point! The power-point is that practical place where theory becomes action. Without a power point even the most learned physicist can't make an electric "fridge" go, while with a power point even the simplest savage can.

Important and Practical

Similarly, there is a sense in which the doctrine of the Means of Grace is the most important and practical of all doctrines, because it is here that all the mysteries of the Faith are "focused," that is, are applied, translated into action, and made available as life and power. (Of Luther's "Six Chief Parts" of the Christian religion, only two do not deal directly with the Means of Grace!) And if it be objected that all this applies to the Means of Grace themselves, not to the doctrine about them, we reply that the right theory of a thing is basic to its proper use. Without the right theory, there can be no power-points at all. And even when there are power points, it still helps to know that they supply not gas or water, nor symbols of electricity, but electricity itself, and of a certain voltage, etc. This is doubly true of the "power points" of God, the Means of Grace: since the life-giving Gospel does not work magically or automatically, but gives its supernatural treasures to faith alone (Romans 3-5; Hebrews 11), it calls for proper, Spirit-given understanding (I Cor. 2), not for uncomprehending superstition.

And doctrinal differences about the Means of Grace have far-reaching consequences for the whole nature and quality of spiritual life, both personal and corporate. Only the right Scriptural teaching about the Means of Grace can lead us safely past the Scylla of externalism, ritualism, sacerdotalism, sacramentalism, etc., and the Charybdis of subjectivism, sacramentarianism, emotionalism, revivalism, and the like, to the vigorous and healthy spiritual life described in the New Testament.

So much for the crucial importance of the subject.

Meaningful Use

Now the "meaningful use" of the Means of Grace depends ultimately on two factors: (1) a realization of our desperate need for God's forgiveness, life, and salvation; and (2) an appreciation of the Word and Sacraments as the divinely appointed means, which not only announce, but actually "sign, seal, and deliver" those heavenly treasures.

We could of course develop this two-fold theme in terms of the general, undifferentiated notion of "the Means of Grace," or "the Word and the Sacraments." But that might be a bit like asking someone to an "intake of carbohydrates," when what is meant is an invitation to tea. And I doubt that even a biochemist, when eating in his unofficial capacity, really prefers "proteins and starches" or even "food" to a tender lamb roast with potatoes and pumpkin!

The point is that the Bible speaks not of "Means of Grace" or even of "Word and Sacraments" in general, but concretely of Baptism, the Gospel, and the Lord's Supper. And while it is certainly not wrong and is often even helpful to use theological short-hand expressions like "Means of Grace" or "Sacraments," it must not be forgotten that this involves the process of abstraction: in treating the two concrete actions of Baptism and Communion, for instance, under the one heading "Sacraments," we must need to think of their COMMON features, and de-emphasize that which is unique, distinctive, and peculiar to each. But though this is useful for certain special purposes in theology, it can be dangerous in the realm of devotion, which thrives on the concrete and hates abstraction. To think, in this latter area, only or even mainly of "Means of Grace" or "Word and Sacraments" in general, is a tragic mistake. The result is an artificial, drab-and-dry sameness in place of the wonderfully generous variety and distinctiveness of our merciful God's gifts of Baptism, the Gospel, and the Communion, as described in the New Testament. It is this drab-and-dry, bloodless, levelling approach which inspires the question: "But if I already have everything through one Means of Grace, why do I need the others?" How utterly foreign to the outlook of the New Testament, which regards Baptism, the Gospel, and the Supper as essential in their own right, each with its own special glory, and none simply as an assembly-line-type "interchangeable part" of the "Means of Grace!"

One Gift of Grace

In this sense, therefore, the Positive theologians of the last century were quite right when they emphasized the uniqueness and distinctiveness of each Means of Grace. But they were very wrong in holding that each Means of Grace conveys an essentially different gift of grace. Thus ONLY Baptism was thought to offer regeneration, and Holy Communion was thought to implant the "germ" of a "Resurrection body" by virtue of which the Christians would rise again on the Last Day! Such nonsense, indeed magic, is nowhere taught or implied in the New Testament, and therefore our own Dr. Francis Pieper, in his great CHRISTIAN DOGMATICS rightly rejected and refuted these claims, as going counter to Scripture and to the Reformation's "sola fide" (by faith alone).

What is different in each Means of Grace is not the gift of grace itself—there cannot be several kinds of forgiveness, life, and salvation, nor are these blessings given in bits and pieces —but the mode or manner of application, and the concrete setting of the act, each with its own "element," function, association of ideas, and significance.

If therefore I shall treat of different aspects of the Christian life in connection with different Means of Grace, I by no means wish to be understood as upholding the absurd errors of the "Positive" theologians. I mean to do nothing different than what we do in the three articles of the Creed, when we attribute Creation to the Father, Redemption to the Son, and Sanctification to the Holy Spirit, even though we of course know perfectly well that all the Persons of the Most Blessed Trinity participate in all three works.

Finally, no one will, I hope, expect anything like a complete or balanced treatment of the Means of Grace, with all their pre-suppositions, implications, and ramifications. That would require vastly more time, space, and knowledge than your scribe possesses. I shall try to do no more than to call attention, within the confines of my prescribed topic, to some aspects of Christian faith and life which seem to me to deserve special mention in our circles. Some brethren may have good reasons for preferring some other selection or arrangement. In that case, "let a good man strike or rebuke me in kindness," Ps. 141:5, as the discussion unfolds.

II. Baptism

There are basically two views of Baptism in Christendom. For convenience' sake we shall call one the "full" and the other the "empty" view respectively. In the "full" view, Baptism actually offers a spiritual gift. It not merely symbolizes, but actually gives forgiveness, life and salvation. It is essentially Gospel, a gracious act of God. In the "empty" view, Baptism is only a picture symbolizing all these gifts, which, however, must be obtained in some other way. Baptism then becomes an act of man and signifies human obedience to divine commands. Baptism so conceived is essentially Law.

The proponents of the "empty" view of course claim that the "full" view comes not from the Bible, but from human tradition and superstition. Actually, the reverse is the case. It is the people who hold the "empty" view, who find that they cannot appeal for support to what the Biblical text actually SAYS. An objective study of John 3:5,6, Acts 2:38, Acts 22:16, Rom. 6:3-5, Gal. 3:26.27, Eph. 5:25,26, Col. 2:11.12, I Peter 3:21 (check Phillips' translation). Tit. 3:5, will show that the New Testament regards Baptism not as a PICTURE but as a MEANS of salvation. Only by explaining the text AWAY and departing from its literal, grammatical sense can one arrive at any other conclusion.

He who holds to the full. Scriptural teaching concerning Baptism, will naturally find much joy, comfort, and strength in his own Baptism. He will meet every onslaught of the Evil One with Luther's triumphant "Baptizatus sum" (I am baptized)! Because I am baptized, therefore I am in Christ, and sin, death, and Satan cannot harm me. Though they accuse me, God loves me, has justified me, and will also accept me on Judgment Day. Baptism means that God is for me; but "if God be for us, who can be against us?" (Rom. 8:31) Moreover, Baptism is not the kind of passport that must be renewed from time to time, or which ceases to be in force. Our Baptism is valid forever, and we may return to it throughout our time of grace here on earth. It is not so that after "shipwreck" Baptism is no longer effective, and some other "second plank" must be sought to cling to. Baptism offers us permanent citizenship in the City of God, and so long as we claim it by faith, we have it.

The True Apostolic Faith

Most significant is St. Paul's inspired assertion (Eph. 4:5), that there is "ONE Lord, ONE Faith, ONE Baptism". It means that every valid Baptism commits one to the ONE Lord, and the ONE true Faith. If the Lutheran Church is the one which teaches this true Faith, in accordance with the Scriptures, then it follows that all Christians, no matter in which denomination they have been baptized, have been baptized into that pure, Scriptural, evangelical Faith which nowadays goes by the nickname "Lutheran." Baptized Christians who later in life find the Church of the pure Word and Sacraments, therefore, are not denying their Baptism, but fulfilling it, coming home where they belong! The Lutheran Church does not wish to peddle some sectarian specialties, Luther's personal notions, and the like. It wishes only to represent faithfully that full, true Apostolic Faith to which the whole Christian Church is committed by Baptism.

There is another famous saying of Luther's which follows from the Scriptural doctrine of Baptism: "Whatever has crawled out of Baptism, may boast that it is already ordained priest, bishop, and pope" (St. Louis edition, X, 272). This is based of course on that Magna Carta of Christian liberty, 2 Peter 2:9: "you are a chosen people, priests of a King, a holy nation, a people saved to be His own" (Beck's translation).

This glorious text, one of the battle cries of the Reformation, was quoted very often by Luther and later by Dr. C.F.W. Walther. It certainly teaches that there are not two classes of Christians, priests and laymen, but only one priestly class. Every Christian, not only the public servant of the Church, has been ordained in Baptism to be a fulltime, 24-hour a day, 7-days a week priest of the Triune God, with all the privileges and responsibilities which this implies.

Christian Liberty

The unregenerate flesh of course cannot understand this wonderful text except in the sense of a carnal democratism, which breeds an un-Christlike, quarrelsome preoccupation with one's own "rights." This sense is foreign to the "mind of Christ" which is to "be in" us (Phil. 2:5). What earthly right can he care for who has the heavenly right to imitate his Savior's divine humility, to take up his cross and follow Him (Matt. 16:24), to lose life in order to find it (v. 25), to serve, and not to be served (Matt. 20:28)? All worldly self-assertion is repugnant to the baptized priest of Christ, who is called to turn the other cheek, sacrifice his cloak too, and walk the second mile (Matt. 6:39-41), to forgive seventy times seven times (Matt. 18:22), to wash one another's feet (John 13:14), to bear injustice patiently a Cor. 6:7, I Pet, 2:19-24). Christian liberty is not carnal license. It is the freedom of those who celebrate their liberation from that dreadful tyrant and taskmaster, sin, whose wages is death (Rom. 6:15-23). Free from sin, they find true liberty not in pleasing themselves, but in pleasing and serving their God, as the Apostle writes: "As free, and not using your liberty for a cloak of maliciousness, but as the servants of God" (I Peter 2:16).

What then is the priestly work into which we have been baptized? It is "to tell of the wonderful deeds of Him who called you out of darkness into His marvelous light" (I Pet, 2:9),

Saved for Something

In other words, salvation is something essentially positive. We are saved not merely FROM something, but above all, FOR something! One of the clearest, most wonderful statements of the very essence of the Gospel, to be found in the whole Bible is Eph. 2:8.9: "You are saved by a gift of love you get by faith. You didn't do it. It is God's gift. It isn't because of anything you have done, or you might boast." Yet this is immediately followed by this statement: "He has made us what we are, creating us in Christ Jesus TO DO GOOD WORKS, WHICH GOD LONG AGO PLANNED FOR US TO LIVE IN" (9 v. 10, Beck's translation, my capitals). This new life, devoted entirely to God and His Kingdom is precisely what EVERY Christian has been baptized into:

"Should we go on sinning so that God may love us all the more? Certainly not! We died to sin. How can we live in it any longer?

"Or don't you know that all of us who were baptized into Christ Jesus by our baptism share in His death? Sharing in His death by our baptism, we were buried with Him so that as the Father's glory raised Christ from the dead, we too will live a new life. If we were united with Him to die as He did, then we'll also rise as He did. We know our old self was nailed with Him to the cross to stop our sinful body and keep us from serving sin any longer. When we're dead, we're free from sin. But if we died with

Christ, we believe we'll also live with Him because we know that Christ, risen from the dead, will not die again. Death has no hold on Him anymore. When He died, He died to sin once, never to die again, and the life He lives He lives for God. So you, too, because you are in Christ Jesus, think of yourselves as dead to sin and living for God" (Rom. 6:1-11, Beck).

Bearing Fruit

There is a great deal of unspiritual, negative thinking in this area. Many appear to believe that Baptism, Justification, Faith, Regenerating are the end, purpose, and finish of the thing. Actually, they are only the beginning! The New Testament Christian never thinks: "Well, I have arrived now, since I have faith and am justified!" (Quietly aside:) "God must be very pleased that I have accepted His offer and allowed Him to save me!" No! The New Testament Christian says: "Now that, thank God, I have been baptized and justified, I can really begin to live a useful life in Christ, the true vine (John 15), Lord, let me bear much fruit for You, all the time, and more and more!"

That same strange, negative thinking also invades the doctrine of the Church: Many people appear to believe that the Church is a kind of exclusive spiritual health resort, where the "patients" sit about in easy chairs and are waited on hand and foot by servile attendants, whose chief and only function is to please and pamper their thin-skinned majesties in every possible way. And woe to the clumsy fellow who forgets his place and displeases by word or action!

What a Satanic caricature of the New Testament picture of the Church! We are called to serve, not to be served; to please the Lord, not ourselves; to advance the interests of His kingdom, not our own!

"And He gave us some men to be apostles, some to speak the Word, some to tell the good news, some to be pastors and teachers, IN ORDER TO GET HIS HOLY PEOPLE READY TO SERVE AS WORKERS AND BUILD THE BODY OF CHRIST till all of us get to be one as we believe and know God's Son, reach a mature manhood, and grow to the full height of Christ . . .He makes the whole body fit together, unites it by every contact with its support, and to the extent that each part is working He makes the body grow and builds it up in love" (Eph. 2:11-16, Beck. See also I Cor. 12:4-31).

No Self-Centered Religious Club

The Church in the Book of Acts is not a lazy, cozy, pampered, spoiled, self-centered religious club, but a fighting, testifying, sacrificing, suffering, loving, dying Church! "Like a mighty army moves the Church of God"! What a joke that is in many cases!

If only Christians would realize what a tremendous cause they've been baptized into, there wouldn't be nearly so much smug self-satisfaction. There would be a tremendous realization of the vastness of the challenge, and of our appalling shortcomings and sins. WE WOULD BE DRIVEN TO GOD, IN HIS GOSPEL AND HIS OTHER SACRAMENT, with urgent pleadings for more mercy, more power, more love, more faith, more understanding, more zeal, more holiness!

People who simply live a decent life and "don't do anybody any harm" are not yet leading Christian lives. Producing the fruits of the Spirit (Gal. 5:22), living the Beatitudes, spreading Christ's Kingdom by word and action, crucifying the flesh, praying constantly, helping the needy, the lonely, the sick, loving the unlovely, these are the marks of genuine Christianity.

Away with dead respectability! Let us have the life which shares Christ's cross and shame—but also His Victory!

Then too we shall have plenty of occasion to comfort ourselves with the wonderful promises of Scripture—and not abuse these by whining and whimpering in neurotic self-pity overall kinds of aches and pains and injuries, real and imagined, which have nothing to do with real bearing of our cross!

The Christian Church, even when she is persecuted and oppressed, is not gloomy, defeatist, and tearful, but joyful, brave, and quietly triumphant in the Lord. That too is our heritage in Baptism!

No indeed. Baptism is not an ending, but a beginning. When the Lord said: "It is finished," He did not mean that we might as well be dead! He meant that His work was finished, so that our life could begin in earnest. Go forth Christian soldier, in the strength of your Baptism!

III. THE GOSPEL

1. Strictly speaking there is really only one Means of Grace, and that is the Gospel. This Gospel then takes different forms. It comes to us as spoken, written, etc. Word, and in a different form, as signed, or sealed Word, in the Sacraments. The Gospel itself remains primary. It is, as Luther often points out, the Word which gives substance and meaning to the Sacraments. This Word of the Gospel, however, alone and of itself, that is, apart from any Sacraments, carries all spiritual power, and imparts the Holy Spirit, forgiveness, and all other blessings. Thus St. Paul writes to the Corinthians that he had been sent to them not to baptize, but to preach the Gospel (his assistants no doubt performed the Baptisms), and that he had personally baptized no one but Crispus and Gaius, and the household of Stephanus (I Cor. 1:14-17). Yet the same Apostle calls himself the spiritual father of the Corinthians: "for in Christ Jesus I have begotten you through the gospel" (4:15). That Gospel "is the power of God unto salvation to everyone that believeth" (Rom. 1:16).

2. This Gospel must be clearly distinguished from the Law. Both Law and Gospel must be constantly applied to us, lest we sink either into smug pride and presumption or into despair and hopelessness. Anyone who has studied Dr. C.F.W. Walther's great classic *Law and Gospel* — which cannot be recommended highly enough—will know that the proper distinction and application of Law and Gospel is not something which is easily mastered in five minutes. It is a Spirit-taught art, learnt in the hard school of prayer, study, and spiritual afflictions, and requires a life-

long application.

No Lazy Man's Pillow

If we start neglecting the Law, the Gospel soon disappears too! Where the dreadful diagnosis is forgotten, even the sweetest medicine soon falls into disuse. And the Gospel, so precious to tortured consciences, parched for the waters of divine mercy and forgiveness, must ever be used to comfort the penitent— but never to make the impenitent comfortable in their impenitence! That would be casting pearls before swine. Those who walk proudly and securely, satisfied with themselves and their spiritual condition, and do not with fear and trembling seek first the Kingdom of God and His righteousness, must be clearly told that they are not Christians but unbelievers and hypocrites, who have no part in the Kingdom of Christ. "Salvation by grace alone through faith alone" must never become a lazy man's pillow, upon which to sit and relax in false comfort and security! Faith alone saves, indeed, but saving faith is never alone! Even the thief on the cross, though converted only moments before his death, was full of holy zeal, confession, and thus good works, from the moment of his conversion! Too many Lutherans show by their lukewarm, spiritually sloppy and careless way of life that they have a false and twisted trust in "salvation by grace alone," thus turning God's gracious life-giving offer into a "savior of death unto death" (2 Cor. 2:16) for themselves! "Whosoever doth not bear his cross and come after Me, cannot be My disciple!" (Luke 14:27)

3. The Gospel is doctrine. This may seem terribly obvious to us, but it is almost universally denied today. While orthodox. Biblical theology, together with our Confessions (Augsburg Confession, VII, for instance), freely speaks of the "doctrine of the Gospel," modern Liberal theology, having rejected the authority of Holy Scripture, knows no such things as definite, God-given doctrine, but only human "interpretations," opinions, and the like. The "Gospel" therefore is regarded as somehow floating above and beyond all these—more or less mistaken and sinful — "interpretations." This irrational mysticism, though it is really the unbelief and skepticism of Satan ("Yea, hath God said?"

Gen. 3:1) and Pontius Pilate ("What is Truth?" John 18:38), often likes to cover its nakedness with Biblical-sounding expressions and phrases. But it is all sham and hypocrisy. The fact is that the Savior sent His Church to teach definite doctrine, Matt. 28:19 ff., not to palaver endlessly about human "insights," and the like. And He promised His truth to His Church, John 8:32. Theology therefore is supposed to be men of God speaking to His people about Him. Instead, it has become a matter of learned gentlemen writing for learned gentlemen about learned gentlemen!

Always Controversial

The fact that the Gospel is doctrine means that it is always controversial. A non-controversial Gospel is no Gospel. The Gospel cannot be some safe, slick slogan, on the wording of which all agree, though each provides his own interpretations, presuppositions, and implications! Though the doctrine of Redemption and of Justification is the heart, soul, and kernel of the Gospel, this nucleus cannot exist apart from the whole body of doctrine: Unless, for instance, the authority of Scripture as sole doctrinal norm, the Fall of Man, as presupposition of the Redemption, and the Trinity, as well as the Person and Work of Christ are maintained, all talk of a "Gospel" or the "grace of God," or the "Christ-event" is mere mummery and illusion.

It is not sufficient, then, to pay lip-service to some pious-sounding slogan: The whole body of Scriptural doctrine hangs together with the Gospel, and must be confessed by those who honor Christ, Mark 8:38. And He promised that those who take His Word seriously, will bear shame and suffering, as He did, for the disciple is not greater than the Master, Matthew 10. Therefore Luther writes that "things are not well with a preacher, if he has peace and isn't attacked by anybody. It is a sign that he doesn't have the right doctrine" (St. L. ed. V, 1125). Elsewhere Luther writes:

"If I profess with the loudest voice and the clearest exposition every portion of the truth of God except precisely that little point which the devil and the world are at that moment attacking, I am not confessing Christ, however boldly I may be professing Christ. Where the battle rages, there the loyalty of the soldier is proved, and to be steady on all the battlefields besides is merely slight and disgrace. If the soldier flinches at that point, it is inexcusable!" (Quoted in *The Faithful Word*, 1965, no. 2, p.1)

A Preaching House

4. Luther says somewhere that the Christian Church is not a "writing-house" but a "preaching-house." God ordained not that everyone should simply get a Bible and read it, but that His Gospel should be preached, by living men of flesh and blood, I Cor. 1:21. When these men, called by God through His Church, proclaim the saving truth of Scripture, it is Christ Himself speaking: "He that heareth you heareth Me; and he that despiseth you despiseth Me" Luke 10:16. No matter how simple or plain the man of God may appear to be, when he proclaims the oracles of God, I Pet. 4:11, it is to be received with all reverence and awe, as from God Himself. And to preach God's Word does not mean simply stringing as many Bible texts together as possible: that is reading, not preaching. Preaching means applying concretely and specifically, to our situation, what the sacred text says. As Christ used illustrations from nature and daily life (yeast, coins, clothes, weddings, agriculture, wineskins, taxes, sheep, etc.) to make His points, so His modern servants have a million sermon illustrations at hand from modern, complex life, to bring home the ancient truths. That of course will bring opposition from those who prefer being lulled to sleep by familiar sounding verbal rituals, and who deeply resent being disturbed in their slumbers by the sudden intrusion of the Gospel into their comfortable modern life! But the real children of God will rejoice to have the Word of God proclaimed in modern

language. Discipleship is for the Twentieth Century too!

An Active Bible Class

5. No Christian individual or congregation can be spiritually healthy without a great deal of Bible Class, led by the pastor, or some other qualified person under his direction. We need to break down that silly "Confirmation complex" which thinks that once a person has been "done," he knows enough and needn't learn any longer. The true Christians always remain teachable. He doesn't harden himself in a stubborn know-it-all attitude. He wishes to be a student, not a master of the Scriptures. And there is so much to be learned from that inexhaustible fountain of truth! So much to be applied!

It is as St. Augustine said somewhere: Holy Scripture is like an ocean which is shallow enough for a child to wade in, and deep enough for an elephant to drown in! We are never finished with it. It remains "profitable for doctrine, etc." (2 Tim. 3:15 ff) till the day we die. And the more we experience of life, of the world, of sin and grace, of holiness and affliction, and of godly controversy, the more interesting does our Bible study become.

In the Introit for the first Sunday after Easter we hear: "and like newborn babies, thirst for the pure milk of the Word so that you'll grow till you're saved" (1 Pet. 2:2, Beck). Do we have that thirst, or have we lost our spiritual appetite? Do we want to learn and understand God's Word, do we yearn for explanations, instructions for this situation in life and that? Do we pray for light from above?

As every person knows, newborn babies do not mildly and patiently indicate that they wouldn't refuse a bit of milk! (If they didn't go to any more trouble to get their milk than many church people do to get God's Word, not many of them would survive!) No, they cry, scream, and finally bellow, ever more insistently, until their urge has been satisfied. And so it is with the Christian and the Word of His God: he cannot live without it. He must read, study, ponder, learn, and apply it every day, and especially every Lord's Day. If we do not know this consuming thirst for God's Word, then let us go back to our schoolmaster, the Law.

Let it drive us to our knees, and open our eyes to the desert of death which surrounds us, that we may learn again to hunger and thirst for righteousness, that we may be filled with the Bread of Life, Whose words are spirit and are life (St. John 6:63)!

One of the best aids toward meaningful Bible study is a New Testament in modern English. Dr. Beck's translation is the best I know of. Phillips' paraphrase is very good too. The Revised Standard Version and the New English Bible and some other versions have dangerous doctrinal errors.

IV. The Communion

A friend of mine recently expressed rather strikingly a wide-spread attitude to public worship.

He said the Christian churches and their people reminded him of an army who were forever parading and saluting, but never getting on with the job of soldiering! A lot of people feel that way. They think that real Christianity is found in the quality of one's daily life (an attractive but misleading half-truth), and that attendance at public services is just a bit of ceremonial "saluting" which is quite harmless for those who are so inclined, but which has very little if anything to do with the real heart of Christianity. And it should be said in all justice that most churches don't do anything on Sunday mornings which might serve to dispel such notions! As the churches empty, and the youth "drifts" away, religious leaders turn to vulgar entertainment in a desperate attempt to attract at least some attention, under pretenses no matter how false!

Our Lutheran churches in Australia, in this tremendously climactic moment of their history, are about to receive, after years of painstaking labor on the part of a joint liturgical committee, the final version of the committee's recommended new Liturgy. It is therefore most fitting just at this time that we should ask ourselves some very basic questions about the meaning of our worship in general, and of the new Liturgy in particular. If the public worship of the Church is to "make sense" to the people and draw them back regularly, it cannot be left to look after itself, and to develop like a cancer, without principles, order, rhyme or reason. Edifying public worship requires a solid "theory," or scheme, which makes sense, and which reflects in the best possible manner the real nature of true Christianity.

It is in this light therefore, that we shall look at that solemn act, established by Christ Himself, which is the central and distinctive feature of Christian worship, which is in fact, according to the very Words of Institution, the New Testament in action!

In this section I shall keep my own comments at a minimum, and simply let the great teachers of the Church speak for themselves. In the first place, to counteract a certain funeral approach to the Sacrament, let us hear some testimonies to the tremendous richness and fullness of this Means of Grace:

Luther

Let Luther begin:

"In conclusion, now that we have the right interpretation and doctrine of the sacrament, there is great need also of an admonition and entreaty that so great a treasure, which is daily administered and distributed among Christians, may not be heedlessly passed by. What I mean is that those who claim to be Christians should prepare themselves to receive this blessed sacrament frequently. For we see that men are becoming listless and lazy about its observance. A lot of people who hear the Gospel, now that the pope's nonsense has been abolished and we are freed from his oppression and authority, let a year, or two, three, or more years go by without receiving the sacrament, as if they were such strong Christians that they have no need of it . . .

"When a person, with nothing to hinder him, lets a long period of time elapse without ever desiring the sacrament, I call that despising it. If you want such liberty, you may just as well take the further liberty not to be a Christian...

"If you choose to fix your eye on how good and pure you are, to work toward the time when nothing will prick your conscience, you will never go...

"In this sacrament he offers us all the treasure he brought from heaven for us, to which he most graciously invites us in other places...Surely it is a sin and a shame that, when he tenderly and faithfully summons and exhorts us to our highest and greatest good, we act so distantly toward it, neglecting it so long that we grow quite cold and callous and lose all desire and love for it. We must never regard the sacrament as a harmful thing from which we should flee, but as a pure, wholesome, soothing medicine which aids and quickens us in both soul and body. For where the soul is healed, the body has benefited also. Why, then, do we act as if the sacrament were a poison which would kill us if we ate of it?...

"Suppose you say, 'What shall I do if I cannot feel this need or experience hunger and thirst for the sacrament?' Answer: For persons in such a state of mind that they cannot feel it, I know no better advice than to suggest that they put their hands to their bosom and ask whether they are made of flesh and blood. If you find that you are, then for your own good turn to St. Paul's Epistle to the Galatians and hear what are the fruits of the flesh...In short, the less you feel your sins and infirmities, the more reason you have to go to the sacrament and seek a remedy...

"If you could see how many daggers, spears, and arrows are at every moment aimed at you. You would be glad to come to the sacrament as often as possible. The only reason we go about so securely and heedlessly is that we neither acknowledge nor believe that we are in the flesh, in this wicked world, or under the kingdom of the devil" (Large Catechism).

Chemnitz

Martin Chemnitz, one of the authors of the Formula of Concord:

"For in the Eucharist we receive the most certain and most excellent pledge of our reconciliation with God, of the remission of sins, of immortality, and of future glorification... For the Son of God in the Eucharist testifies, by means of the most excellent and most certain pledge, that is, the distribution of His body and blood, that He certainly imparts Himself to the individual using this Sacrament in faith, and applies and seals the remission of sins, reconciliation with God, and His other benefits, which He acquired for the Church by the giving of His body and the shedding of His blood, that they might be offered by Word and Sacrament, and received by faith" (*Examen.* 303. 306).

"For in that Holy Supper we eat the body of Life, which is the most efficacious antidote against death; concerning which Christ Himself promised, John 6:54: 'Whosoever shall eat of My flesh, and drink of My blood, the same hath eternal life, and I shall raise him again on the last day.' For this reason the old Fathers called the Holy Supper of the Lord an *eohodion* and *viaticum* (travelers' food supply. K.M.), which is necessary for those who are journeying out of this mortal life. Thus both Irenaeus and Chrysostom based the hope of their resurrection on this that in the Supper they had become participants in the body of Him, over Whom death hath no more dominion, Rom. 6:9" (*Harmony of the Four Gospels*, I,749).

Gerhard
John Gerhard, great Lutheran champion of the 17th century:

"For what more evident and more illustrious testimony of His love could He leave us, than that He instituted, in the Eucharist, His own body to be eaten and His own blood to be drunk? Christ instituted this Sacrament when He was about to enter upon His passion and to do battle against the devil, death, and hell. Therefore there is no stronger weapon against the enemies, no more excellent medicine against our spiritual weakness, against devil, no more salutary viaticum (travelers' food supply, K.M.) for those departing out of this world, than the most holy Sacrament of the Eucharist. Christ instituted this Sacrament when He was about to depart from His Apostles through death. Therefore He instituted it for this purpose, that it might be the most efficacious means through which He might unite and conjoin to Himself, as closely as possible, the Apostles and all true believers . . .

"For what more living and efficacious remembrance of Christ's death could there be than that which takes place in us by means of the Communion with the body given into death for us and the blood shed for us?" (*Harmony*. II, pp. 1084.1102).

Walther
Dr. C.F.W. Walther, founder of the Missouri Synod, U.S.A.:

"Woe to us, therefore, if we wanted to yield and give in here! Thereby we would be surrendering nothing less than the Holy of Holies of the Christian Church, the Ark of the Covenant and the Mercy Seat of the New Covenant. . .

"It is true, my beloved in the Holy Supper there is given to us no other grace than that which is given to us already in Baptism, in the preaching of the Gospel, and in the comforting Absolution . . . Accordingly it might well seem as if every person is thereby sufficiently supplied with the treasure of the forgiveness of sins and that it therefore matters little, if the Holy Supper with its forgiveness of sins is mutilated or taken from him entirely.

"But this is by no means so. Rather, the Holy Supper is the real crown of all the means of grace which Christ has given to His dear Christendom. . . O, who can express what a glorious, comforting, heavenly sweet Meal the Holy Supper is? Here the forgiveness of sins is not only preached, proclaimed, promised, assured, and sealed to us, as in the other means of grace, but here Christ at the same time gives His Body and His Blood to His Christians, as the guarantee of it . . . No, a more precious, incontrovertible divine guarantee there cannot be. . . Let us not be ashamed of this doctrine, but joyfully confess it, and publicly praise it as the most precious treasure entrusted to us " (Maundy Thursday sermon on I Cor.

11:23-32, in *Amerikanisch-Lutherische Evangelien Postille*, p. 147).

Scriver
Christian Scriver:
"We in no way detract from the other means of grace. Holy Baptism, the Word, and faith; we do not want to sunder what God hath joined together; God also has other foods, beside bread, which, eaten by man, strengthens and preserves his body, yet bread is the noblest. What is begun in Holy Baptism, and through the Word, that is confirmed and as it were completed in the venerable Supper; the highest degree which a baptized and believing Christian can reach in the mystery of fellowship with Christ, is without a doubt the one which is granted him in this holy Meal of Love. And I know nothing that would be more powerful in strengthening and preserving faith, and bringing it to full joy and highest pleasure, than just this Sacrament" (*Seelenschatz*, I, 756).

Krauth
Finally, Charles Porterfield Krauth, the greatest English speaking Lutheran theologian America has produced:
"The Sacramental Presence is the necessary sequel, the crowning glory of the Incarnation and Atonement . . . All theology without exception has had views of the atonement which were lower or higher, as its views of the Lord's Supper were low or high. Men have talked and written as if the doctrine of our Church, on this point, were a stupid blunder, forced upon it by the self-will and obstinacy of one man. The truth is, that this doctrine, clearly revealed in the New Testament, clearly confessed by the early Church, lies at the very heart of the Evangelical system—Christ is the center of the system, and in the Supper is the center of Christ's revelation of Himself. The glory and mystery of the Incarnation combine there as they combine nowhere else. Communion with Christ is that by which we live, and the Supper is '**the** Communion.' Had Luther abandoned this vital doctrine, the Evangelical Protestant church would have abandoned him. He did not make this doctrine—next in its immeasurable importance to that of justification by faith, with which it in dissolubly coheres—the doctrine made him. The doctrine of the Lord's Supper is the most vital and practical in the whole range of the profoundest Christian life—the doctrine which, beyond all others, conditions and vitalizes that life, for in it the character of faith is determined, invigorated, and purified as it is nowhere else. It is not only a fundamental doctrine, but is among the most fundamental of fundamentals. We know what we have written. We know that to take our Savior at His Word here, to receive the teachings of the New Testament in their obvious intent, is to incur with the current religionism a reproach little less bitter than if we had taken up arms against the holiest truths of our faith. We are willing to endure it . . .The Lutheran Church has suffered more for her adherence to this doctrine than from all other causes, but the doctrine itself repays her for all her suffering. To her it is a very small thing that she should be judged of man's judgment..." (*Conservative Reformation*. 1963 ed., pp. 650,655,656).

The Place of Holy Communion

Now, what is the place of the Holy Communion in the public worship of Christian Church?

From the Book of Acts we know that the Christians of the Apostolic Church "continued steadfastly in the Apostles' doctrine and fellowship, and in breaking of bread, and in prayers," Acts 2:42.

Dr. C.F.W. Walther writes:

"The first Christians celebrated it almost daily; especially in times of persecution. In order to be daily ready for death...The Holy Supper was regarded as the most glorious divine Armory, in which one receives the most invincible weapons for the spiritual battle ... The holy Supper with the body and blood of Jesus Christ is the new Tree of Life, which stood in Paradise, which Christ has now again planted in His Kingdom of Grace. O adorable, comforting mystery! The holy flesh of God, which the angels adore and the archangels reverence, becomes a Food of sinners! Let the heavens rejoice, let the earth be glad, but still more the believing soul, which enjoys such great Gifts!" (Maundy Thursday sermon, Gnadenjahr, pp. 209ff).

And the great Australian Lutheran theologian Dr. H. Sasse says:

"This close connection between the proclamation of the Gospel and the Sacrament of the Altar explains the fact that at all times the Eucharist has been the center of the Church's worship and life. . . . Thus this sacrament was in every respect the life of the Church. It was never to be separated from the Gospel. The Church of the first centuries was the Church of the Eucharist. A Sunday, a Lord's Day, was unthinkable without the Lord's Supper. But if ever the Church was a preaching Church, the Church of the apostles and the Church Fathers was. The same is true of all great periods of the Church. The sacrament and the sermon belong together, and it is always a sign of the decay of the Church if one is emphasized at the expense of the other" (This Is My Body, p. 2).

Every Sunday

The Lutheran Church at the time of the Reformation kept the historic order of service, known as "the mass," but cleansed it of all abuses and superstitions. But the basic framework of a service with Word and Sacrament was kept and celebrated every Sunday and holy day, according to Article XXIV of the Augsburg Confession and its Apology.

And that is still the Service we have today.

Unfortunately F. Lochner's classic "Hauptgottesdienst" (The Main Service) is not available in English. Lochner was, together with C.F.W. Walther, one of the leaders of the Missouri Synod. He was also a liturgical scholar. In his book he said, among other things:

"On the basis of Acts 2:42 and I Cor. 11 and according to the example of the ancient Church, the Lutheran Church regards the Communion Service as the most glorious and important of all public services ... She therefore distinguishes between the Main Service, and Minor Services. A divine Service becomes the Main Service not by virtue of the significance of the Sunday or the holy day, nor because of the season of the year, nor through liturgical elaboration, but, as given by the Scriptural relation of Word and Sacrament, *by* virtue of the fact that the action of the Sacrament of the Body and Blood of Christ immediately follows upon the proclamation of the Word of the Gospel, and thus represents the seal of the Word, the aim and conclusion of the Service. All other services, in which the action of the Sacrament is not intended from the outset, become Minor Services, no matter how richly they have been liturgically appointed in the past" (p. 6).

The only major English work on this subject is L. Reed's *The Lutheran Liturgy*, but it contains theological weaknesses. Nevertheless, it is regarded as the standard book, and contains a wealth of information of the origin and significance of Lutheran liturgical forms. A very helpful popular treatment of the Service is contained in the little green booklet, *Our Way of Worship*. A good devotional treatment of the Sacrament is Pastor Fields' *Communion with Christ*, a recent Concordia paper-back. In places one could wish for a stronger Confessional stand, but as a whole the book may be warmly recommended.

Word and Sacrament

Although this is not a matter of doctrine, it will be interesting to note the conception of the Christian Service as presented, for instance, in the *Apology of the Augsburg Confession*, one of the Confessional documents which all Lutheran pastors are sworn to uphold:

"To begin with, we must repeat the prefatory statement that we do not abolish the Mass but religiously keep and defend it. In our churches Mass is celebrated every Sunday and on other festivals, when the sacrament if offered to those who wish for it after they have been examined and absolved...

"We are perfectly willing for the Mass to be understood as a daily sacrifice, provided this means the whole Mass, the ceremony and also the proclamation of the Gospel, faith, prayer, and thanksgiving. Taken together, these are the daily sacrifice of the New Testament; the ceremony was instituted because of them and ought not be separated from them. Therefore, Paul says (I Cor. 11:26), 'As often as you eat this bread and drink the cup, you proclaim the Lord's death.'" (XXIV,1.35).

It was clearly the intention of the Lutheran Church to preserve intact the historic Christian Service, with its twin "peaks" of Word and Sacrament.

Martin Luther himself, when asked for advice as to how often Holy Communion should be celebrated, replied, under date of August 15, 1528: "that one or two masses be held in the two parish churches on Sundays or holy days, depending on whether there are many or few communicants..."

"... during the week, let mass be held on whatever days it would be necessary, that is, if several communicants were there, and would ask and desire it. Thereby no one would be forced to the Sacrament, and yet everyone would be sufficiently served therein" (St. Louis edition, X, 2256-2258).

Note that Luther is stating not the legalistic principle that Christians must receive the Sacrament weekly, but the evangelical principle that the Sacrament should be available to those who desire it, at all times.

May Not Must
So long as the whole subject is approached with the question: "How often must I come?" It is being thoroughly misunderstood. It is not a burdensome duty, a "must," but a wonderful evangelical gift and privilege, a "may"! To a hungry boy the call to tea is a most welcome invitation, not an obnoxious command! And that is precisely the attitude of the Christian to that great Feast prepared by Christ Himself!

Nor is the situation seen correctly as the need of so many individuals, which might just as well be satisfied in a series of private Communions. The Communion is by its very nature a public corporate, congregational act, and is so treated in the New Testament, I Cor. 10 and 11. Private Communion, for the sick, is an exception due to necessity, not the rule of what is normal and desirable.

Our old theologians were strongly aware of this New Testament emphasis on the corporate aspect of Holy Communion. Dr. C.F.W. Walther's great edition of Baier's Compendium, a standard manual of orthodox theology, quotes John Gerhard as listing among the "less principal purposes" of Holy Communion: "4. That we might preserve the public assemblies of the Christians, the strength and bond of which is the celebration of the Lord's Supper, I Cor. 11,20" (III. 529).

And elsewhere Gerhard has written:

"Because therefore it has been accepted as a practice in the Christian Church, that in the public assemblies of the Church after the preaching and hearing of the Word, this Sacrament is celebrated, therefore this custom must not be departed from without urgent necessity... it is ... clear from Acts 20:7, I Cor. 11:20.33, that when the Christians did gather at one place, they were accustomed to celebrate the Eucharist" (*Harmony*, II, 0185).

The Missouri Synod's entire early (and orthodox!) theological literature, up to World War I, was summarized and collated in Eckhardt's REAL LEXICON. This work says, under "Abendmahl" (Lord's Supper):

"The Lord's Supper ought to be administered publicly and corporately, because
   (a) Christ and the Apostles did it that way.
   (b) Because the Lord's Supper is a public confession; proclaiming the Lord's death, I Cor. 11, but a proclamation does not usually happen in a corner.
   (c) Because it is a tie of fellowship." Communion. I Cor. 10:17: One Body.

Note (a) The place of the celebration is therefore the Church, the Assembly Service (Versammlungsgottesdienst) of the Christians.

Note (b) It is just in the celebration of the Lord's Supper that the Main Service finds its culmination point" (p. 43).

A Lutheran Service?

Questions we should face honestly and seriously if our life in the Means of Grace is to be as meaningful as possible, would no doubt include also these: Is there such a thing as "the Lutheran Service"? If so, what is it? Could it just as easily be something else? What is our guide in liturgical matters? Is it only our own habit and custom? Do we want things done a certain way because we can see that this is best in principle, or simply because that's what we're used to? Should we seriously reconsider the frequency of opportunities for Holy Communion in our congregations, particularly in the light of Apostolic and ancient as well as Reformation practice? Are our times less dangerous to Christian faith than earlier times, and do we therefore have less need of the Sacrament, or are we less spiritual? Can we adopt an "I don't care" attitude toward the standard practice of the Church before our times, without incurring St. Paul's rebuke: "What? Came the Word of God out from you? Or came it unto you only?" (I Cor. 14:36)? Quite aside from habits, customs, and traditions, which are only secondary, what would be the best possible practice NOW? What would best edify the Church? Where there is a pastor available, is there any reason why the full Main Service should not be celebrated at each regular Sunday gathering of the congregation? Is the doctrine of the Real Presence as it were "dead theory" in our devotional life, or is it living practice? Does it make for a striking difference in our church life, as distinguished from the practice of those churches which do not believe in the Real Presence? Can the "drift of youth" from the Church be arrested in part by making the Service more obviously vital and meaningful? How?

V. Conclusion

The "possession and use" of the pure Word and Sacraments is a most blessed, but also a very dangerous thing. To whom much is given, from him shall much be required. The Corinthians relied on having Baptism, and Communion, and felt safe in this "possession and use." St. Paul sharply rebuked them, reminding them that all their forefathers were baptized, in a way, and ate of Christ—yet with many of them God was displeased, and they perished, I Cor. 10.

For the convinced Christian the Sunday Service is not like saluting and parading, but like the diver's "life-line," his oxygen supply, without which he cannot survive. Forgiveness of sins, power for the new life and work for Christ, joy in suffering, peace in trouble, fellowship with God and the fellow-believers, in short everything is there to be found where God through Word and Sacrament creates and supports that Colony of Heaven, that Paradise on earth, the holy Christian Church! "Awake, Thou Spirit, Who didst fire the watchmen of the Church's youth!" (Hymn 24)

Lutheran News, June 27, 1966, July 11, 1966, August 8, 1966

1. The decisive difference among churches is about ____.
2. What leads us past the Scylla of externalism and the Charybdis of subjectivism? ____
3. There is only ____ gift of grace.
4. All three persons of the Trinity participate in ____.
5. In the "empty" view Baptism is only ____.
6. The New Testament regards Baptism not as a ____ but as a ____ of Salvation.
7. What is the Magna Carta of Christian liberty? ____
8. We are not saved merely ____ something but above all ____ something.
9. We are called to ____ not to be ____.
10. What are the marks of genuine Christianity? ____
11. Baptism is not an ending but a ____.
12. What is the only Mans of Grace? ____
13. What book cannot be highly recommended enough? ____
14. Saving faith is never ____.
15. Modern Liberal theology knows no such thing as ____.
16. Theology is supposed to be men of God speaking to His people about ____.
17. Preaching means applying ____.
18. Real children of God will rejoice to have the gospel proclaimed in ____.
19. What is the "Confirmation complex?" ____
20. The Revised Standard Version and the New English Bible and some other versions have ____.
21. Charles Porterfield Krauth was the ____ theologian America produced.
22. How often should the Lord's Supper be celebrated? ____

LITURGICAL COMMONPLACES

April 30, 1979

It is no secret that Lutheranism in America is in the throes of a profound crisis. But times of crisis must be seen as times of opportunity. When a tired old order breaks up there results a state of flux which encourages a brisk competition of ideas. Decisions taken at such times, before the concrete hardens as it were, can set future courses for decades, perhaps centuries. These generalities find ready application in the whole liturgical sphere, and particularly in our Missouri Synod. On the one hand, deviations from past norms, embodied in *The Lutheran Hymnal*, of 1941, have assumed epidemic proportions and constitute what may well be described as a state of chaos. On the other hand, the rejection of the current inter-Lutheran efforts at liturgical consensus leaves Missouri quite free to consider the whole thing afresh. It seems obvious that something must and will be done. But what? Much depends on the answer, which should, therefore, not be given lightly or hastily. If the outcome is to be worthwhile, it must be solidly grounded in a careful clarification and re-appropriation of first principles. The observations which follow are respectfully offered simply as one small contribution in this direction. They are meant, moreover, to focus not on technical details—though these can be important—but on meat-and potato issues. The choice between cranberries and horse-radish can always be made later.

I. Liturgical Substance

Most churches in the Western world are facing a decline in church-attendance. The trend may gallop here and creep there, but its direction seems relentlessly downward. It is our duty as churchmen to ponder deeply the reasons for this trend. Otherwise we may be tempted to respond with the absurd superstition of believing, in C. S. Lewis' words, that "people can be lured to go to church by incessant brightenings, lightenings, lengthenings, abridgments, simplifications, and complications of the service."[1] Let us take the bull by the horns and listen to a rather representative "Memo to a Parson, from a Wistful Young Man":[2]

> Let me tell you the main reason I don't attend anymore, or at least not regularly. Since leaving home to go out on my own, I've visited all kinds of churches, but they all seem just about the same. All of them strike me as being about as enervating as a cup of lukewarm postum. When I go to church, what do I hear? From the pulpit, a semi-religious version of what Kenneth Galbraith calls "the conventional wisdom." From the choir loft, incredible Victorian anthems—"the kind that Grandma used to love." From the pew, the attitude you discover at alumni reunions— "Where there's not a single dry eye, but nobody believes a word of it." And from the boutonniered ushers, the kind of mechanical handshake which makes me suspect that they would greet

Jesus at the Second Coming by saying: "It was nice of you to come." In short...the average church stands as a perfect symbol of nearly everything I despise—false gentility, empty sentiment, emotional impoverishment, intellectual mediocrity, and spiritual tepidity. Maybe it's my pride speaking, but I just don't want to be identified with an institution like that.

We could of course comfort ourselves by saying that the Lutheran church is surely different, that the caricature is overdrawn, and that the young man in question was being not simply wistful but even silly in discarding gems of great price on account of shabby packaging. But that would only keep us from trying to understand the situation. Few experienced pastors will deny that in general, the young man's perception of church services is widely held, also in Lutheran circles, although it is not often consciously articulated. For many, services are uncomfortable formalities to be endured with Stoic resignation.

It is tempting at this point to rail against modern materialism and hedonism, golf, the media, Sunday outings, and fishing trips. No doubt these weighty matters offer not a few occasions for penitence, although we cannot pursue them here. Rather more relevant to our topic is a problem which is not often discussed: our Wistful Young Man probably has no clear idea at all of what a proper church service *ought* to be like. Nor, it seems, do the churches he visits have any compelling theory of what they are about on Sunday mornings. He and they may, indeed, cherish some misty vision of what ideal worship would be like, but they are not very clear in the head about it. This fuzzy-contoured vision, moreover, afflicts not only so-called "fringe-members." How else can one explain the fact that practicing, otherwise well-instructed Lutherans seem to feel free to miss church for perfectly frivolous reasons, e. g., Sunday dinner guests—not to speak of pastors who do not attend church while on holidays because they are "resting"? In an age like ours, when weekends are full of the clamor of secular trivia, and material delights beckon on every side, Christians require an unusually clear and compelling "theory" of congregational worship. "Hearing the Word of God" was once a weighty phrase, corresponding to an awesome reality. Today, in the thinking of many, the whole thing can be taken care of without inconvenience or loss of time, if need be, by tuning in to the "Lutheran Hour" while devoutly chewing Kentucky Fried Chicken on the way to Six Flags!

The notion of "worship" in popular Protestantism does not seem to suggest anything so formal as a church service. It is more likely to be associated with rousing choruses of "How Great Thou Art," either at a Billy Graham rally or in a rugged setting out of doors, preferably round a campfire, holding hands. Mawkish gimmickry of various kinds is marketed as making for "effective" worship. Church services themselves, however, are seen as rather drab and dreary on the whole. They tend to be viewed not as banquets but as menu-reading sessions. (This impression, by the way, is reinforced by the lavish distribution of printed matter.) How many people would bother to go to a restaurant just to read the menu? Here, it seems to me, lies the heart of the difficulty. It is not as if people thought they should have dinners but grumblingly accepted menus instead. They expect only menus—with flowers, candles, and musical settings perhaps—but still only menus! Richard Wurmbrand, having noted the frequent refrain in church-bulletins that refreshments will be served after the service, asks pointedly: "Why do you not provide refreshment in the service?" On this point at least those outside and many inside the churches are agreed. It is just that the insiders have learned to derive a sense of satisfaction and mutual approval from uncomplaining performance of the menu-reading duty. Repelled by this bloodless, Law-oriented, moralizing religiosity, multitudes seek solace in the murkiest mumbo-jumbo and readily fall prey even to celluloid absurdities like "Close Encounters of the Third Kind," of which a recent reviewer wrote:

> The thoroughness of the film's surrogate spirituality is revealed in the final scene, depicting the appearance and "landing" of the UFO's. The huge "mother ship" looks less like a space vehicle than a vast city of light descending from the heavens. Whether the parallel is deliberate or not, Spielberg's offer of this ersatz New Jerusalem (cf. Revelation 21) as the answer to Mankind's spiritual longings is a slick con-job indeed. Roy Neary's "conversion" under a beam of bright light while on the road to Crystal Lake is said to have been consciously modeled after St. Paul's conversion on the road to Damascus.[3]

As Chesterdon observed: If people don't believe in God, they will not believe in nothing—they will believe in anything!

Advancing now from menus to soups, let us consider C. S. Lewis' pertinent argument:

> We may *salva reverentia* divide religions, as we do soups, into "thick" and "clear". By Thick I mean those which have orgies and ecstasies and mysteries and local attachments: Africa is full of Thick religions. By Clear I mean those which are philosophical, ethical, and universalizing: Stoicism, Buddhism and the Ethical Church are Clear religions. Now if there is a true religion it must be both Thick and Clear: for the true God must have made both the child and the man, both the savage and the citizen, both the head and the belly. And the only two religions that fulfil this condition are Hinduism and Christianity. But Hinduism fulfils it imperfectly. The Clear religion of the Brahmin hermit in the jungle and the Thick religion of the neighboring temple go on *side by side*. The Brahmin hermit doesn't bother about the temple prostitute nor the worshiper in the temple about the hermit's metaphysic. But Christianity really breaks down the middle wall of the partition. It takes a convert from central Africa and tells him to obey an enlightened universalist ethic: it takes a twentieth century academic prig like me and tells me to go fasting to a Mystery, to drink the blood of the Lord. The savage convert has to be Clear: I have to be Thick. That is how one knows one has come to the real religion.[4]

Christianity is "Thick" in Lewis' sense in two closely related respects. First of all, there is the redemptive mystery of the Incarnation itself: God made Man for our salvation. Or, in J.B. Phillips' memorable phrase, God has "come into focus" for us in Jesus Christ. Holy Scripture sets before us not vague wafflings about an anonymous cosmic Blur—the great Mush-God, as he has been called, for born-again politicians of all world-religions —but the concrete, historical, yet eternal Person in Whom "the fullness of the Godhead dwells bodily" (Col. 2:9). So much so that, as Luther comments on this text, whoever will not find God there in Christ, will never find Him anywhere else, even if he were to go above Heaven, under Hell, or into space!

Secondly, just as God is "focused" for us in Christ, so Christ in turn is effectively "focused" in His life-giving Gospel, including Holy Baptism and the Sacrament of the Altar. These blessed Means of Grace are not mere pictures, symbols, or reminders—as our whole Reformed environment suggests —but real and powerful communicators of all the redemptive riches of Christ. This life-giving, faith creating, "dynamic of God for salvation," as St. Paul calls the Gospel in Romans 1:16, can never be reduced to a mere menu: it is the Messianic Feast itself. Indeed, one might distinguish within the Gospel yet two further modes of "Thickness": the washing of regeneration in Baptism and the Real Presence of Christ's Body and Blood in the Holy Supper. Of the latter Charles Porterfield Krauth has written:

> The principles of interpretation which relieve us of the Eucharistic mystery take from us the mystery of the Trinity, the Incarnation, and the Atonement. . . .Christ is the Centre of the system, and in the Supper is the center of Christ's revelation of Himself. The glory and mystery of the incarnation combine there as they combine nowhere else. Communion with Christ is that by which we live, and the Supper is "the Communion."[5]

Both the God-in-Christ and the Christ-in-the-Gospel themes are united in the profound simplicity of the words of St. John: "This is He Who *came* by water and blood, even Jesus Christ; not by water only, but by water and blood. . . .And there are three that bear witness in earth, the Spirit, and the water, and the blood: and these three agree in one" (I Jn. 5:6,8). These great and mysterious realities define, constitute and shape the whole nature of Christian worship. That worship is concrete and sacramental, not vague and spiritualizing. It is not a pseudo-occult mysticism seeking by means of devotional techniques and exertions to penetrate and conquer the barrier between heaven and earth. All such man-made attempts, with all their impressive psychic fireworks, cannot escape from the gravitational field of sinful creatureliness. They deal only with human projections and demonic mirages. The whole point of the Incarnation and of the Means of Grace is that fellowship with God takes place on His terms alone, and that means for the present here on earth, on our level. It is He Who has broken through the Great Divide from His side, in order to give Himself to us graciously on ours.

Even at this point, however, the Lutheran understanding of worship can still be aborted by means of a facile doctrinaire schematism which thinks abstractly of "Means of Grace" or "Word and Sacraments," rather than concretely of Baptism, preaching, absolution, and Eucharist. It is a Calvinistic doctrine that all sacraments must be alike. This idea is developed by the *Admonitio Neostadiensis,* for example, in its attempt to refute the Formula of Concord's confession of the Real Presence in the Eucharist. Replying to this Calvinistic attack, the Lutherans Chemnitz, Selnecker and Kirchner point out with almost tedious repetitiousness in their *Apology or Defense of the Christian Book of Concord* (see especially Chapter V) that the unique nature of each Sacrament must be determined not by appealing to theoretical generalizations, but by paying attention to the actual biblical texts, particularly the respective words of institution. If the Means of Grace were mechanically interchangeable, rather than organically ordered, it would make sense to say: "Today we have Baptism and, therefore, we do not need Communion." Such an argument, however, is quite impossible. It should be equally impossible to argue: "As long as we have preaching regularly, and the Lord's Supper occasionally, the Means of Grace are in action, and all the rest is adiaphora." What must be seen is that in the Lutheran Confessions as in the New Testament the Eucharist is not an occasional extra, an exceptional additive for especially pious occasions, but a regular, central and constitutive feature of Christian worship. Preaching and the Sacrament belong together not anyhow, or helter-skelter, by statistical coincidence, but as mutually corresponding elements within one integrated whole.

Of the practice in apostolic and sub-apostolic times, Oscar Cullmann has written in his book, *Early Christian Worship,* as follows:

> The Lord's Supper is thus the basis and goal of every gathering. This corresponds to all that we have already determined about the place and time and basic character of the primitive Christian gathering. . . .Accordingly, it is not as though early Christianity had known three kinds of service, as we are in the habit of imagining, following the modern example: service of the Word and, alongside of it. Baptism and the Lord's Supper. It is rather so: in the early Church there are only these two celebrations or services—the common meal, within the framework of which proclamation of the Word has always a place, and Baptism . . . The *Lord's Supper* is the natural climax towards which the service thus understood moves and without which it is unthinkable, since here Christ unites himself with his community as crucified and risen and makes it in this way one with himself, actually builds it up as his body (Cor. 10:17).[6]

In respect of the Lutheran Confessions an extraordinary development seems to have taken place. Even those sections of world Lutheranism which have cultivated a strong consciousness of Article X of the Augsburg

Confession and its Apology, are hardly aware of its practical implementation and ramifications in Article XXIV. The tendency has been to maintain the Sacramental Presence as a matter of doctrine, but to let the practice of the Sacrament drift from its central position in the church to a more peripheral, supplementary status, as in the Reformed pattern. The strong corporate, communal implications (I Cor. 10:17) have been largely lost. This is not the view of the Lutheran Confessions. Article XXIV of the Augsburg Confession and of the Apology sees the Mass or Liturgy as consisting of preaching and the Sacrament, and as something to be done every Sunday and holy day. Nor is this merely a temporary accommodation. Luther himself, for instance, in his Latin Mass of 1523, defined the mass as consisting, "properly speaking," of "using the Gospel and communing at the Table of the Lord." In fact, he rejects, in the same work, the Roman custom of omitting the Consecration on Good Friday, and says that this is "to mock and ridicule Christ with half of a mass and the one part of the Sacrament."[7] To the city of Nuremberg he recommended, upon request, under date of August 15, 1528,

> that one or two masses be held in the two parish churches on Sundays or holy days, depending on whether there are many or few communicants.... During the week, let mass be held on whatever days it would be necessary, that is, if several communicants were there, and would ask and desire it. Thereby no one would be forced to the Sacrament, and yet everyone would be sufficiently served therein.[8]

Significant for the corporate understanding of the Sacrament is this paragraph of the Apology (XXIV,35):

> We are perfectly willing for the Mass to be understood as a daily sacrifice, provided this means the whole Mass, the ceremony and also the proclamation of the Gospel, faith, prayer, and thanksgiving. Taken together, these are the daily sacrifice of the New Testament; the ceremony was instituted because of them and ought not be separated from them. Therefore Paul says (I Cor. 11:26), "As often as ye eat this bread and drink this cup, you proclaim the Lord's death."

This, too, was the understanding of the classical Lutheran theologians. Gerhard, for instance, is quoted in Dr. C. F. W. Walther's expanded edition of Baier's *Compendium* to the effect that one of the "less principal purposes" of the Sacrament is "that we might preserve the public assemblies of the Christians, the strength and bond of which is the celebration of the Lord's Supper (I Cor. 11:20)."[9] Elsewhere Gerhard wrote:

> Because it has been accepted as a practice in the Christian church that in the public assemblies of the church after the preaching and hearing of the Word this Sacrament is celebrated, therefore, this custom must not be departed from without urgent necessity ... it is ... clear from Acts 20:7; I Cor. 11:20,33, that when the Christians did gather at one place, they were accustomed to celebrate the Eucharist.[10]

This deeply sacramental understanding of worship is also expressed quite explicitly in the literature of the early Missouri Synod, e.g., F. Lochner's *Hauptgottesdienst*. Eckhardt's *Reallexicon* (1907-1917), an ambitious topical summary of the Synod's published theology, makes the following points under *"Abendmahl" (Lord's* Supper):

The Lord's Supper ought to be administered publicly and
corporately, because
  (a) Christ and the apostles did it that way;
  (b) The Lord's Supper is a public confession, proclaiming the Lord's death (I Cor. 11), but a proclamation does not usually happen in a corner;
  (c) It is a tie of fellowship. Communion. I Cor. 10,17: One Body.

Note (a) The place of the celebration is therefore the Church, the corporate worship *(Versammlungsgottesdienst)* of the Christians.
Note (b) It is just in the celebration of the Lord's Supper that the Main Service finds its culmination point *(Gipfelpunkt)*.

The same source says under *"Gottesdienst"* (Divine Worship) that for the Lutheran Reformation there were
various services: Preaching services. Catechism services. Vesper services. — A Main Service *(Hauptgottesdienst)* was a service with the Lords Supper. All others were minor services *(Nebengottesdienste)* . . . Minor services were: Matins, early on Sundays before the Main Service; Vespers on Saturday afternoon (Catechism sermon). . .

There follows a separate section on "The Lutheran Order of Service," enumerating the various parts, beginning with the Introit and ending with the Lord's Supper, which "is the seal of the Word and therefore follows the sermon." Of this specific order it is stated: "The Lutheran Order of Service is a unit with a fine integration of its parts" (ein *Ganzes in feiner Gliederung)*. This Service was "corrupted. . . (1.) by the Thirty Years War; (2.) by those of Spener's persuasion (Pietists) . . .; (3.) by Rationalism."

The foregoing clearly suggests that the most urgent liturgical need is not for this or that ceremonial detail: what is needed is the restoration of the Lutheran understanding of the close bond between sermon and sacrament. "The sacrament and the sermon belong together," wrote Sasse, "and it is always a sign of the decay of the church if one is emphasized at the expense of the other."[11] This is clearly not a question of tinkering with fussy bits and pieces of the liturgical machinery, but one of regaining a sense of the organic whole. Where the Service is understood not as a central sermon-core surrounded by fluffy festoons of trivia, but as the church's awesomely objective participation in the very life-giving Mystery of Salvation, there not only will penitent sinners gladly throng the courts of the Lord, but pastors themselves will understand their sacred office more clearly and will be less tempted either to abandon that office altogether or else to escape into all sorts of secondary roles and functions in search of identity and "fulfilment."

It is not, of course, to be expected that simply publishing a new liturgy and hymnbook will achieve all this. But it could certainly help. A new hymnbook could, for instance, follow the example of the Missouri Synod's official *Kirchen-Agende* published by Concordia Publishing House in 1902, in offering only one main Sunday service, the Order of Holy Communion, which then ends after the Sermon with prayers, blessing, and hymn, in case the Communion is not celebrated. At least this would avoid the false impression created by the "Page Five" form, that the main service of the church is complete without the Sacrament. If such a denatured form, a Communion Order without Communion, must be given independent status, then let it, at the very least, appear last, not first. Also, the close and indissoluble connections between liturgy and dogma make it highly desirable that the Small Catechism and the Augsburg Confession be printed in full in any future hymnal.

II. Liturgical Form

One hesitates to enter the whole field of external forms, where tastes and habits are so easily roused to furious combat. Yet the following four sets of "commonplaces" suggest themselves as particularly relevant to our modern Lutheran situation:

(1) On the one hand, in the matter of genuine adiaphora one must cultivate a truly evangelical and ecumenical breadth of perspective (FC SD X, 31). If the Lutheran Church is serious about representing, not sectarian whims, but the pure Gospel of the one, holy, catholic, and apostolic Church of Christ, then she cannot in principle wish to squeeze the devotion of Zulus and Spaniards, Chinese and Americans, Brazilians and New Zealanders, all into one narrow sixteenth century Saxon groove! In this sense, there cannot be such a thing as *"the* Lutheran Liturgy." The unchanging content must be the Gospel of God, but the form must of necessity be colored by the Christian history of each of the world's nations, tongues, cultures, and continents. Here and now we must concentrate not on liturgies in general, or on some pseudo-cosmopolitan hotchpotch, but on a form or forms suitable to an English-speaking specifically North American, environment.

Granted the substance, then, form is relatively indifferent. But only relatively. "Surely," asks C. S. Lewis, "the more fully one believes that a strictly supernatural event takes place, the less one can attach any great importance to the dress, gestures, and position of the priest?"[12] The argument holds only for a choice among equally acceptable alternatives. For surely nobody would care to complete C. S. Lewis' sentence like this: "The more fully one believes that a strictly supernatural event takes place, the less one can attach any great importance to whether the celebrant is dressed in jeans or smokes cigarettes at the altar." Obviously it does matter a great deal whether the words and actions of celebrant and people are in harmony with the sacred transactions which they must express and convey. It is, indeed, an adiaphoron whether the Introit is spoken or chanted. It does not follow, however, that the Introit may, therefore, be spoken or chanted indifferently, negligently, or perfunctorily. *That* can never be an adiaphoron.

The trouble is that actions do often speak louder than words. If either words or actions do not express the sense of the Liturgy, the Service of Word and Sacrament, or even run counter to it, then they are no longer adiaphora. A traditionalist Roman Catholic observed very perceptively of the post-Vatican II liturgical changes that a doctrine like the Real Presence can be materially altered and even surrendered without any explicit pronouncement, simply by a more permissive ceremonial (e.g., heedlessly dropping particles of consecrated bread to the ground). Even in daily life words, actions, and situations are perceived as jarring or even grotesque if they are not in keeping with one another. To plead for mercy before a human court, for instance, while remaining seated, hands in pockets, and chewing gum would be insufferable. It seems even more incongruous for a clergyman to sit down comfortably during the Kyrie or the Gloria in Excelsis, legs crossed so as to give maximum exposure to canary colored socks, and gaze into the congregation to see who is there. Or consider the disruptive effect of hackneyed "traffic directions" being given every few minutes: "We now continue our so-and-so with this or that found on page such-and-such, in the front, middle, back, etc., of your hymnbook!" Imagine what a total disaster it would be if a stage manager were constantly to interrupt a gripping drama by appearing on stage to make announcements like these: "Ladies and gentlemen, will you now please turn to page 285 of your paperback edition of *Four Great Plays by Henrik Ibsen. . .*" "As it is very hot today, please skip pages 158 to 176. We continue with Act III of 'An Enemy of the People,' line three, at the top of page 177." If even the presentation of mere fiction and make-believe forbids all sorts of disruptive rehearsal chatter, how much more the very embodiment of the living, eternal truth? Verily there is here One greater than Shakespeare or Ibsen! His minister, therefore, who leads the People of God in the celebration of the mysteries of His New Covenant (I Cor. 4:1), has no right to sound as if he were announcing Walt Disney mummeries to tired tourists for the twenty-millionth time!

In the choice of equally suitable forms, then, let mutual tolerance and accommodation prevail. We must, indeed, beware of the misguided zeal with which St. Augustine of Canterbury forced his Roman rite on the representatives of a more ancient form of British Christianity. But once a fitting form has been chosen, it needs to be filled not with casual indifference, but with awe and reverence, with that fear and trembling which befit the presence not only of angels and archangels and of all the company of Heaven, but of the Adorable Divine Majesty Himself. It is in this sense that we must understand the Augsburg Confession's paradoxical admonition about adiaphora: "Nothing contributes so much to the maintenance of dignity in public worship and the cultivation of reverence and devotion among the people as the proper observance of ceremonies in the churches" ("Of Abuses," Introduction, 6).

(2) The worship of God is not a means to an end (e. g., "evangelism"), but is an end in itself. It is in fact *the* ultimate purpose of the church (Eph. 1:12.14; Phil. 1:11: 2:10,11: I Peter 2:5), and must give meaning, direction, and impetus to all particular functions and activities of the church, including the great missionary task (Matt. 28:19.20). The means that the church's public liturgy, that is, the Service of Word and Sacrament, dare not be treated as a public relations exercise, as these words are usually understood. The idea, for instance, that the Service should be "meaningful," that is, clear and obvious to any casual visitor who might pop in from the street, is shortsightedly pragmatic. A "service" tailored to such a misguided ideal would comprise a *mélange* of threadbare banalities, which even the casual visitor is likely to find unbearable after the third time—not to speak of the faithful who attend regularly for threescore years and ten. People who come to the church seeking divine truth do not expect it to be huckstered like soap or soft drinks, with mindless jingles. Indeed, they respect the church's uncompromising celebration of mysteries which are not at once transparent to the uninstructed. A few years ago, for instance, an American lady walked into a Russian Orthodox monastery in New York State, and was so impressed by the service in church Slavonic, of which she did not understand a word, that she promptly willed all her wealth to that monastery, saying that here alone had she found people who really prayed!

By far the greatest missionary magnetism in the Service, however, has always been exerted by good evangelical preaching. This dare never be forgotten, least of all in that church which confesses in the *Apology* (XV, 42,43):

... the chief worship of God is the preaching of the Gospel. When our opponents do preach, they talk about human traditions, the worship of the saints, and similar trifles. This the people rightly despise and walk out on them after the reading of the Gospel. . . In our churches, on the other hand, all sermons deal with topics like these: penitence, the fear of God, faith in Christ, the righteousness of faith, prayer and our assurance that it is efficacious and is heard, the cross, respect for rulers and for all civil ordinances, the distinction between the kingdom of Christ (or the spiritual kingdom) and political affairs, marriage, the education and instruction of children, chastity, and all the works of love.

And again we assert (XXIV.50,51):

Practical and clear sermons hold an audience, but neither the people nor the clergy have ever understood our opponents' teaching. The real adornment of the churches is godly, practical, and clear teaching, the godly use of the sacraments, ardent prayer, and the like. Candles, golden vessels, and ornaments like that are fitting, but they are not the peculiar adornment of the church.

Liturgy is the worship and distribution of Christ in Word and Sacrament. Using outward forms and aesthetic appeal as excuse or cosmetic for vapid, incompetent, dogmatically wobbly preaching is an empty parody; it is mere ritualism. Good, sound, solid preaching is by far the most important and the most demanding task of the ministerial office. It is in fact *the* apostolic work *par excellence* (Acts 6:2,4; II Cor. 3; I Tim. 5:17). Who indeed is sufficient for these things? Only God can make able ministers of the New Covenant (II Cor. 2:16; 3:6). Pastoral competence, however, requires spiritual and theological exercise, growth, and progress (I Tim. 4:7,15). Proper pastors' conferences (not insipid "church-workers" and families kaffeeklatsches) are vital in this process, and growth in the quality of preaching ought to have top priority on the agenda. This means continuous concentration not primarily on techniques but on content. The electronic media particularly are so effective in shaping a secular mentality, even among church-people, that Christian preachers must labor strenuously to counter and exorcise these demons. They must constantly build and reinforce a soundly, uncompromisingly Christian perspective. Preaching is this sort of spiritual battle for men's minds and souls. It is not an anemic recitation of pat formulas and clichés. That is merely sermonizing. Preaching is the ever-fresh exposition and application of God's living Word for today. The point, as someone has well said, is not to illuminate the obscure biblical text with the light of clever scholarship, but to let the light of the text (Ps. 119:105) illuminate our lives!

People do hunger and thirst for authentic proclamation. When the Soviet priest Dimitri Dudko included a question and answer session in his celebration of the Liturgy, the church could scarcely hold the crowds that gathered. These sessions proved so popular that the KGB arranged an automobile "accident" which, fortunately, Father Dudko survived, though with broken legs. The craving for the Bread of Life is not limited to the Soviet Union. Westerners are more jaded, it is true. But the hunger is there nevertheless.

(3) A third set of commonplaces has to do with what C. S. Lewis called the "Liturgical Fidget." I can do no better than to quote Lewis directly:

> Novelty, simply as such, can have only an entertainment value. And they don't go to church to be entertained. They go to *use* the service, or, if you prefer, to *enact* it. Every service is a structure of acts and words through which we receive a sacrament, or repent, or supplicate, or adore. And it enables us to do these things best—if you like, it "works" best—when, through long familiarity, we don't have to think about it. As long as you notice, and have to count, the steps, you *are* not yet dancing, but only learning to dance. A good shoe is a shoe you don't notice. Good reading becomes possible when you need not consciously think about eyes, or light, or print, or spelling. The perfect church service would be one we were almost unaware of; our attention would have been on God. But every novelty prevents this. It fixes our attention on the service itself; and thinking about worship is a different thing from worshipping. . . . There is really some excuse for the

man who said, "I wish they'd remember that the charge to Peter was. Feed my sheep, not try experiments on my rats, or even teach my performing dogs new tricks."

Thus my whole liturgiological position really boils down to an entreaty for permanence and uniformity. I can make do with almost any kind of service whatever if only it will stay put. But if each form is snatched away just when I am beginning to feel at home in it, then I can never make any progress in the art of worship. You give me no chance to acquire the trained habit—*habito dell'arte.* [13]

What then shall we make of the idea that "the youth" get bored with sameness and therefore require constant innovations to keep them interested? The sentiment is well-meaning enough but is essentially misguided. It is true that initially some silly youngsters (by no means all) may enjoy having the service turned into a variety show, especially one that is flattering to the inane Youth Cult images promoted by the media for profit. In the long term, however, such an approach is bound to produce conscious or subconscious contempt for the church. Who, after all, could respect an institution, which is after two thousand years' experience, so confused about its functions as to say, in effect: "Dear children, help us! We are no longer sure about what we ought to be doing. Perhaps you might have some good ideas?" Who could possibly take seriously the play-worship prefixed with that horrid word, "experimental"?

The fact is that no healthy, viable society lets its children arbitrate its values. It is for the elders of the tribe to guard its cultural heritage and to transmit it solemnly to the younger generation—never *vice versa.* Also in our society the problem is not with the youth but with their elders. If youth are confused about values, it is mainly because their parents are. If the liturgy is boring to children it is usually because the parents do not find it very interesting either. If children saw adults treating the Sunday Service as the most important activity of their lives, they would respect it too, and would never dream of treating it as a pop-event, to be tinkered with by every Tom, Dick, and Harry. A church which has won the conscientious loyalty of parents-particularly fathers (Eph. 3:15; 6:4)!—will have the devotion of their children too. But a church which abjectly capitulates to the whims and tastes of adolescents will have, and deserve, neither.

Finally, there is a variety-principle built into the liturgy, and that is the rhythm of the church-year. The basic units of this gentle, natural rhythm are the week and the year. This cycle is virtually broken by forcing onto it the alien drum-beat of "monthly emphases" based on the activistic, organizational imperatives of the financial year. It is also broken by the false off-on or even off-off-off-on *staccato* of "Communion Sundays" and "non-Communion Sundays." The proper change from Sunday to Sunday should be in the specific meaning and application of the Sacrament, not in having or not having it. The Eucharist is the whole Gospel in action. This one Gospel, like a precious diamond, has many facets or aspects, of which one or two are especially highlighted in each Sunday's or festival's Gospel pericope. And through whatever concrete facet the full Gospel is celebrated on a given day that is the specific meaning, or the mode of application of the Sacrament on that day. The Sacrament is always the full Gospel-gift, of course. But on Christmas Day we receive it under the aspect of the Lord's Nativity, on Epiphany in celebration of His Baptism, on Laetare Sunday as the Divine Bread of Life revealed in the miraculous feeding of the multitude, and so on. In other words, the Sacrament, like the Gospel itself, must never be seen as someone narrow aspect or some unvarying "standard ration" in the feast that is Christianity. It is rather the whole reality, under many wonderful aspects, each especially observed and celebrated at various times. Each time it is as new and fresh as are the daily mercies of God. We have here the Kaleidoscope of God, which, at each weekly or seasonal tilt, exhibit the same divine generosity in ever new and exciting configurations.

(4) In conclusion, something should be said about the twofold requirement that liturgical and musical forms be (a) solemn and fitting and (b) congregationally singable. The early church studiously avoided the music characteristic of the ostentation and voluptuousness of pagan state religion and mystery cults. Sobriety, not frenzy, was the mark of Christian worship, I Cor. 12:2; Eph. 5:15-20. In our own time it is difficult to imagine a more appalling travesty than a "service" or "hymns" reeking of the pagan debaucheries and obscenities of the "rock"-cult. It is sheer mockery to turn the Christian mysteries into raucous night-club acts. What has Light to do with Darkness, Christ with Belial, or the Agnus Dei with the Beatles, Monkees, and their ilk? The solemn celebrations of the church (I Cor. 5:8; Heb. 13:10) must not be defiled with the modes and manners of Canaanite fertility religions (I Cor. 10:7.8) and of their modern counterparts.

A fitting reverence, however, is one thing; a snobbish stuffiness is quite another. Good church music must be singable. And what was singable once is not necessarily singable today. Moreover, what sounds majestic when sung by thousands in a Gothic cathedral, may sound merely ludicrous when attempted by seventeen people to the funereal wailings of an electronic organ-simulator. The church must cultivate living devotion, not exquisite museum-pieces to delight sophisticated musical palates. It is better, therefore, to sing "My Faith Looks Up To Thee" with zest and gusto, than to devastate a great hymn like "Isaiah Mighty Seer" by stumbling painfully and clumsily about its craggy grandeur. This is not to suggest by any means that the old treasures should now be abandoned. The question must, however, be handled with some discretion. Congregations can and should learn to sing the great Christian classics of the past. But the Sunday Service is not the time or the place for practice and rehearsal. It is discouraging for a congregation to be compelled to sing five unfamiliar hymns in a row. Most of the hymns sung on a given Sunday should be sufficiently well-known to be sung truly corporately and with fervor. It is sufficient to cope with one or two unfamiliar hymns per service. This allows for the necessary training without destroying the congregation's joy in worship. It should also be borne in mind that, given a fitting and stable liturgical framework, there is considerable scope within it for popularly expressive hymns (CA XXIV, 2). One would be hard put to suggest a more perfect embodiment of these principles than the practice of the great Bishop St. Ambrose of Milan. During Holy Week of the year 386, a year before the conversion of St. Augustine, the dowager empress Justina, who was a fanatical Arian, tried to compel Ambrose to surrender one of his churches to the Arians. This the bishop refused steadfastly to do. Various pressures were brought to bear, including the dramatic encirclement of Ambrose's church by Arian soldiers, who had orders to allow people in but not out. Thus, Ambrose and many of his people were forced to spend several days in the church buildings under virtual siege. To encourage his congregation in the true faith, Ambrose composed beautiful hymns exalting the Blessed Trinity and the true Divinity of Our Lord. These hymns were then chanted antiphonally by clergy and people. Augustine reports that this chanting was so compelling that it was taken up even by Arian soldiers outside! In the sixteenth century, likewise, the Reformation was often sung into people's hearts and minds. Ought not the celebration in our churches today be similarly contagious?

FOOTNOTES

1. C. S. Lewis. *Letters To Malcolm: Chiefly On Prayer* (New York: Harcourt. Brace, and World. 1964). p. 4.

2. Roy Larson. "Memo to a Parson, from a Wistful Young Man." *Religion in Life*. XXXI (19611. p. 356. cited in E. W. Janetzki. "Where Is The Church?" *Basic Studies in Christianity* (Adelaide: Lutheran Publishing House, n. d.). p. 71.

3. *Spiritual Counterfeits Project Newsletter,* Berkeley. California. January-February 1978.

4. C. S. Lewis. *Undeceptions* (London: Geoffrey Bles. 1971). p. 76.

5. Charles Porterfield Krauth. *The Conservative Reformation and Its Theology* (Minneapolis: Augsburg. 1963). pp. 650.655,

6. Oscar Cullmann. *Early Christian Worship* (London: SCM Press. 1966). pp. 30.31.34.

7. Jaroslav Pelikan and Helmut T. Lehmann. eds, *Luther's Works* (St. Louis: Concordia Publishing; House. 1955-1976). 53. p 24.

8. J. G. Walch. ed., *Dr. Martin Luther's Saemmtliche Schriften* (St. Louis: Concordia Publishing House). 10. cols. 2256-2258.

9. C. F, W. Walther. ed., *Johanni Gulielmi Baieri Compendium Theologiae Positicae* (St. Louis: Concordia. 18791. p. 529.

10 Martin Chemnitz. Polycarp Leyser. and John Gerhard. *Harmoniae Quatuor Evangelistarum* (Frankfort and Hamburg. 1662), IL p. 1085

11. H. Sasse. *This Is My Body* (Minneapolis: Augsburg 1959) p. 2.

12. C. S. Lewis. Letters To Malcolm, p. 9.

13. *Ibid.,* pp. 4-6.

From The Concordia Theological Quarterly
Christian News, April 30, 1979

1. Lutheranism is America is in the throes of ____.
2. Most churches in the Western world are facing a ____.
3. Should pastors attend church while "on holidays?" ____
4. What did Richard Wurmbrand observe about "refreshments?" ____
5. Chesterton observed that if people don't believe in God, they ____.
6. It is a Calvinist doctrine that all sacraments are ____.

7. What is needed is restoration of the Lutheran understanding of the close bond between the ____ and the ____.
8. The Small Catechism and the Augsburg Confession should be printed in ____.
9. It is an ____ if the Introit is spoken or chanted?
10. What about "traffic directions" at a worship service? ____
11. The ultimate purpose of the church is to ____.
12. The real adornment of the churches is ____.
13. Liturgy is the worship and distribution of ____.
14. What is by far the most important and demanding task of the ministerial office? ____
15. What should have top priority at proper pastors' conferences? ____
16. No healthy, viable society lets its ____ arbitrate its values.
17. Good church music must be ____.
18. Most of the hymns sung on a given Sunday should be ____.
19. In the sixteenth century the Reformation was often ____ into the hearts of people.

LUTHER'S THEOLOGY OF THE CROSS

May 28, 1984

The suggestion that human reason is competent to establish or at least to support matters of faith, the idea that faith can rest on the accomplishments of human reason and of scientific learning — that thinking has done a great deal of harm. Paley thought that he could prove by this method not only that there is a God, but what kind of God he is, that he is one, that he is benevolent, that he is good. This is a very dangerous assumption. Therefore, I want to go back 300 years before Paley to Martin Luther.

Luther Was Thoroughly Realistic
Luther understood perfectly that human reason can accomplish nothing for faith. He understood that even if human reason can come to the conclusion that there is a God, there is nothing to show that this God is particularly good. In fact, by looking at nature and seeing nature in tooth and claw, one may well consider that God is either evil or indifferent Luther understood that since the Fall into sin, things are not as clear-cut as reason may assume. We cannot base our religion on philosophizing about what we may find in nature. No telescope and no microscope can disclose to us any more than the footprints of God. What he is really like, we can find out only if God steps out of the darkness, so to speak, and makes himself known in his Son; otherwise you are guessing. We may just as well guess, either that there is no God, or that he doesn't care about us.

No Room For Guess-Work
Luther is able fully to anticipate the modern lashing out at God in great anger for allowing the terrible sufferings beginning with World War I and then World War II. Ours is one of the most cruel centuries that ever existed. Shortly before World War I, it was thought that we were on the track of inevitable progress. Things were getting ever better. We were becoming so civilized that Europe would never know war again. We were moving to ever greater progress and final Utopia. Then came World War I. The whole house of cards came down. People said, if that can happen — these nameless horrors of war, all these people dying, all this inconceivable human suffering — there cannot be a God. They rebelled against this easy God based on Paley assumptions, the easy sort of heavenly Father Christmas/Santa Claus God, whose main job it was to maintain minimum levels of jollity in the world. If God didn't do that, if he allowed terrible suffering and terrible tragedy, then he wasn't worthy to be recognized. Either there wasn't a God or he didn't care.

The Tragedy of Evil
Luther understood that fully, and one of his great pronouncements

was this: by this natural sort of means, before God can seem God to us, he must first seem to be the Devil. Behind that lies Luther's deep understanding of the tragedy of evil. He did not believe in the happy-go-lucky world of Paley, who deemphasized the problem of evil. Luther understood that we are caught in a terrible calamity, that we are out of sorts with the will and purposes of our Creator. Cardinal Newman put it in a very interesting way. He said, "If I were to look in a mirror and not see my reflection, I would get the kind of creepy feeling that I actually get when I look into the world — God's world — and fail to find there a reflection of the Creator. It tells me that there is no God — but that is not possible. Since there is a God, then this living, bustling world must in some deep sense be cut off from him. It must be involved with some terrible original calamity. It has lost its way."

Reason Cannot Produce Faith

Luther understood that. He never underestimated the seriousness of sin, the radicalness with which it has destroyed everything. Reason may be very interesting. It may tickle our fancy. It may excite our brain. It may stimulate our philosophical discussion. It may have a great deal of usefulness in the realm of public morality and public culture. But it cannot produce one ounce of faith. Faith must rest on altogether different assumptions. Reason will give us the philosophical notions of God — and leave us dead in trespasses and sins.

The Lowly Things of God

Luther brings this out in his Heidelberg Disputation in 1518 where his famous theses, especially 19 and 20, say this: "Not he deserves to be called a theologian who can understand the invisible things of God as known from the things which have been made. There Luther echoes Romans chapter one exactly. St Paul says that anyone with common sense can deduce that there is a God simply from the created things of the universe. But Luther insists that a person who does merely that, is not yet a theologian. He says that very deliberately, because in the Middle Ages many theologians prided themselves on how much they were able to show with human reason. The impressive thing was — look what reason can do. Faith is a doubtful business; the impressive thing is how far reason can go. Announce a lecture on some way-out subject — flying saucers or some latest scientific evidence — that is fascinating! Announce a Bible study on St. Paul's doctrine of the Church in Ephesians and 3½ theologians may turn up. There is something in the former that tickles our imagination, that appeals to our philosophical reason, that fascinates us. Aware of the danger, Luther insists that is not theology. That is merely philosophy. The true theologian is he who sees and understands the lowly, humble things of God through suffering and cross. That is Luther's theology of the cross.

God Comes to Us In Humble Form

Luther says we are not capable of knowing God as he is by direct knowledge. If God were to face us with the full radiance of his Being, the radiation would kill us. Even the seraphim and cherubim have to hide their faces from the bright light that is God. He is unapproachable. Instead of overpowering us with his unbearable light, this great God comes to us in humble form: the babe at Bethlehem, the man on the cross. He becomes one of us. He hides his glory. He hides himself deeply in human flesh and appears as the unlikely carpenter from Nazareth to weed out all human pride. Even at the beginning of his ministry, Satan tempts him to forsake that lowliness, to take the high road, to take the cheap, sensational, public relations way. Throw yourself down from the temple and you will have everybody at your feet! And the Lord deliberately resists that to take the low road that will culminate in Gethsemane and Golgotha — but then also in the resurrection. This is Luther's theology of the cross: we cannot find God by taking the high road of high-flown speculation.

Everything Must Work For Good
When things go wrong, we need to have access to God. We need to have the knowledge of God in the normal problems of daily life. It is a great embarrassment at times when something goes wrong: innocent children die, the wicked prosper, the good are put down, things seem to happen by chance, —children starve to death, civilians suffer in war — all of this is a great embarrassment. However, if you bring in the problem of evil, it is quite different. If the Savior himself the Son of God, had to go to the cross, then no suffering on earth can really surprise us. We can face it with God's guarantee that he has transformed it by his suffering, not into something pointless, but into something which has the guarantee of God stamped on it: everything must work together for our good.

Promises Attached to a Straw
The devil, says Luther, sets out to blind us with false appearances. He leads us away from God's work to our own impressive spiritual calisthenics. We all attach great importance to our own achievements and merits. But the Scriptures teach that if we pile together all the works of all the monks, no matter how precious and dazzling they might appear, they would not be as noble and good as if God were to pick up a straw. We are so dazzled by great religious spectacle and golden chasubles, lights and incense, all of which are quite good in their own place. But this is nothing compared to when God attaches his promise to a straw. He has virtually done that to a piece of bread on the altar. Luther talks about Baptism as a divine water.

He says:
"Therefore we constantly teach that the Sacraments and all the external things ordained and instituted by God should be regarded not according to the gross external mask, as we see the shell of a nut, but as that in which God's Word is enclosed."

Don't Go By Appearance!

Instead of going by appearance, by the way things look, we go by the Word. Appearance sees nothing much in Jesus of Nazareth. Just another carpenter from Galilee! People who met Jesus in the street did not turn around and say. 'There is God!' There was no halo shining above him. Luther saw that so clearly. He said that God hid himself in the person of our Lord so deeply, so humbly incognito, that on the last day some of his former neighbors from Nazareth will come up to him and say, 'How did you get here? Didn't you build my house?' God comes in this humble way in order to encourage and create faith and humility, not proud ostentation. There is an exact parallel between how God came in Christ and how he comes now in the Means of Grace.

The Decisive Act of Salvation

I believe that this is the central religious problem of our modern world — to the extent that it is still Christian. The problem is this. Here is the event of the cross — never to be separated from the resurrection — let's say roughly AD 30. We are in the year 1984. How do we bridge the gap? The decisive salvatory act, the decisive deed of salvation, has happened in the events of Christ's life, death and resurrection. This is a finished gift. Virtually everybody says that, although not as consistently as they might.

Selling Christianity Short

But then the problem is, how do we get at that today? Here all sorts of tragic ways of selling Christianity short. For instance, people say, "Well, we have to think about it in prayer. We must shut our eyes and think of Jesus." For others there are the revival hymns such as *Come to the Cross* and *Come to Me*. At revival sessions people sing O *Lamb of God, I come, I come*. And when they get there, what confronts them? A decision card, or some other less-than-divine arrangement! Still others say, "Well, it's a matter of meditation. We make it present for ourselves by a mental act of our imagination." The whole thing becomes very fuzzy and vague. This is why you have an atmosphere of groping and yearning, pushing and squeezing. That's not the solution, because that kind of solution can easily lead to despair, to total spiritual and psychic derangement.

All of God Available in Jesus

The real solution is the one that God has provided. The Lord says, "I am the way, and the truth, and the life, no one comes to the Father, but by me". There is no other traffic with God's grace except through this bridge of Jesus Christ. There we meet all of God. "In him the whole fullness of deity dwells bodily. You have come to fullness of life in him." Just as all of God is given in Christ Jesus, his Son — and we can't meet him in any other way than through his Son — so all of Christ is available to us today in the blessed Means of Grace, in the Holy Gospel and Sacraments.

Contact Through the Word

It's not as if we are facing some kind of metaphysical wall and we have to work our way through it and bash our heads against it. And somehow try to get to the other side. No! God breaks through it on his terms. He makes contact through his Word. And the contact is not made somewhere up there in heaven, where we can't go. It's made right here on earth. Christ came to earth. The humble Means of Grace which God has established don't look like much; the Word, preached by sinful human beings; Baptism — a bit of water that doesn't make any halo appear on the baby — it may even scream; bread and wine, which don't look like much — and no chemical analysis of bread and wine will ever yield the conclusion that this is the body and blood of God — a divine transfusion of life and salvation. But, as Luther says, these are the things we know to be there from the Word. And faith goes by the Word, not by sense, experience, excitement, emotion, or whatever. So the gap is bridged. The gulf is crossed by God himself in the means that he has established: Word and Sacraments.

Full Blessing Through the Word

Luther has some striking things to say about this, with which I should like to conclude. He says about the Word, the Gospels, which we read Sunday after Sunday: these pericopes, these Lessons, are not histories — he means they are not only histories —above all they are not dead histories or histories of the dead like other histories, but they are Sacraments, the texts are Sacraments. And he explains what he means: they convey the very thing they talk about. The text is so remarkable; it is alive as no other text, because it is God's Word that conveys the very power of the resurrection in some way that is totally beyond our calculation. Historical investigation and argument can deal only with the tip of the iceberg, the little bit on top that you can see and investigate. But the fullness that no one can see — that is conveyed to us by the Means of Grace. Read, sometime when you have a chance, Luther's word against the heavenly prophets — I think it is in Vol. 40 of the American Edition — who had been saying quite fanatically that the way to get to Christ is by internal struggle and meditation, by participating in the sufferings of Christ.

Go Where Blessing Is Distributed

Luther says, "Bosh! That's not how it's done. It is done by Christ doing it." Then he uses a phrase which probably to us moderns sounds horrible: When I need forgiveness I don't go to the cross, because I won't find it there. Isn't that shocking? How can he not go to the cross? All the evangelists say to us: "Come to the cross". But Luther says, "How can you get to the cross? It's no longer there. And even if it were there, Christ has long since gone from there." He says, No, I don't go to the cross. I run to Absolution or the Sacrament. Why? This is where the cross is distributed.

And then Luther makes this profound observation: "We speak in two ways about the forgiveness of sins: one, where the forgiveness of sins is acquired, and two, where it is distributed. You mustn't confuse these two — they are quite different." On the cross Christ acquired the forgiveness of sins. He won it there; he purchased it, finished it. It's a completed act in a way that neither his Roman opponents nor Geneva could ever understand.

Everything Hinges On This

For Luther, this is a completely finished act of salvation that needs only to be distributed. Christ won it. It's all there. But he didn't distribute it there. He distributes it in the Sacraments. That's why it is so necessary to go into this background of the Means of Grace, the two evangelical Sacraments, Baptism and the Holy Eucharist. They have their origin precisely in this, that they are the means, together with the Word, through which all this reality actually comes to us here and now, wherever we may be. There on the cross Jesus won it. Here he distributes it. Just as there is no other way to God except through Christ, so there is no other way to Christ except through the Means of Grace, the Word and the Sacraments.

The Lutheran, March 5, 1984
Christian News, May 28, 1984

1. What thinking has done a great deal of harm? ____
2. Reason cannot produce one ounce of ___.
3. What is Luther's theology of the cross? ____
4. How is all of Christ available to us today? ____
5. We can't meet God in any way except through ____.
6. Where is the cross distributed? ____

THE SACRAMENT AN EASTER AFFAIR

October 15, 1984

Why did Luther carry on such a vigorous battle for what is in the Sacrament? I draw only one or two themes from the rich New Testament presentation. For instance, think of the Sacrament as the New Testament Passover, where Paul writes in the Easter Epistle, **1 Corinthians 5:7 —** *"Christ, our paschal lamb, is sacrificed"*. This has deep connections with the resurrection, because the New Testament never divides the cross and the resurrection. These are seen as one complete unit. Lutherans, too, need to see that the Sacrament is not basically a Maundy Thursday or Good Friday affair — which it also is. With the Early Church, we need to see that the Sacrament is primarily a resurrection, Easter affair. This is why, as Dr. Sasse points out, the Lord's Day, the day of resurrection, was never complete without the Lord's Supper, the Lord's Word in his Church. These great things belong together. The Early Church made this connection between the Sacrament and the resurrection.

The Resurrection Banquet

In his interesting book, *Early Christian Worship*, Oscar Cullmann points out that the symbol of the *fish* was a symbol not merely for Jesus Christ generally. We all know that the Greek word for fish is made up of the first letters of the words *Jesus Christ, Son of God, Savior*. Cullmann points out that the symbolism goes deeper than that. It goes back to the time when the resurrected Savior comes to the disciples and feeds them with broiled fish. All the resurrection appearances — except the one with the women at the tomb, where it simply wouldn't be practical — occur in connection with mealtimes, in connection with food. A most important, and probably the true variant reading in Acts 1, where it talks about the Lord being with the disciples for 40 days, the Syriac version, says that he took salt with them, that is, he ate with them for 40 days. The point is that the resurrection appearances take place in connection with mealtimes. Remember the Emmaeus road! At the breaking of bread, their eyes were opened and they recognized the Resurrected One. The Sacrament now came to be regarded as the continuation of the resurrection appearances of the Lord. That's very important. As we have it in John 20, on the first resurrection night, the disciples being assembled, the Lord stood among them and said, **"Peace be with you"**. That was at mealtime. They were gathered for dinner. On the following week, the next Lord's Day, he appears again. This time Thomas is there and he confirms his faith. The point is that there is an unbroken chain of Lord's Days going right back to that first one, which was not interrupted by the Lord's Ascension into heaven, and which didn't take him further away, but made him closer to us. He now rules and effectively controls the universe for the benefit of his Church. The Sacrament means specifically the resurrection banquet, where the Resurrected One himself is among us as truly as he was with Thomas and the disciples, and says to us, **"Peace be with you"**.

Joy and Celebration

It is important that we see the Sacrament as a reality of joy and celebration, not simply or primarily a doleful, penitential thing. One dear lady once said, "O pastor, we can't have the Sacrament at Easter, surely. Easter is a time of joy!" She thought that the Sacrament is basically long-faced, grim-faced, and the organists have to drag and sound funereal. But if we see with the Ancient Church that the Sacrament is a feast of the Resurrected One, we shall come, yes, penitently, yes, in sack-cloth and ashes for our sins, but also and above all, rejoicing in the great salvation and in the Resurrected One, because we receive into these bodies which are subject to death (St. Paul: *"Wretched man that I am!* Who will deliver me from this body of death?" — full of death in every way) the living flesh of him, who by his resurrection, has overcome death. By giving his resurrected body, over which death has no more dominion, by giving to our bodies this very flesh that has overcome Satan, death and hell, we have a guarantee that this body, too, will live, despite all appearances to the contrary.

No Shadowy Contact

There is one more dimension to that. It's always very sad that Christians, in time of crisis, can fall prey to the attractions of cultists and occultists of various descriptions, who seem to offer them some kind of strange warmth, weird illumination, and a sense of emotional fulfilment. Why is it for example, at the time of bereavement, many Christians who are perhaps not too established in the faith, actually tempted to go to spiritists? You can imagine how tempting it could be if you have just lost your life-long partner. Afterwards, you think, I should have said that; we should have cleared this up, and there was no chance to do it. How comforting, then, it could be if some dear old soul appears and says, "I know somebody who can make contact. It's not too late. You can still pass your message on to your dear departed one. He or she can speak to you." This can be very tempting to people in their loneliness, to make this sort of shadowy contact, and thus make themselves playthings of demonic forces which take advantage of their sensibilities in this way.

A Blessed Reality - Heaven Is Wide Open

What Satan offers in dreadful distortion and caricature as a shadowy thing in dark corners, that the Church celebrates in broad daylight as a blessed reality, because in the Sacrament, we receive the Resurrected One. Wherever he is, there is heaven. Heaven for us is not a place far away. How many light-years would it take a rocket to get to heaven? It's not a question of light years. Luther points out that Stephen, when he was being killed, saw heaven open, it was right there — without any telescopes. So heaven is right here. It is in a different dimension. God breaks through to us in his Word and Sacrament. Heaven is very close. Heaven is right there, where God makes an opening. As Luther points out in Baptism heaven was rent. It was torn and it stays torn, wherever the Gospel is. Heaven is wide open. Wherever Christ is, there are all our dear ones who have gone before.

One at the Altar

I can never understand why some people, after bereavement, feel they can't come to church. They miss out on so much comfort and consolation. That is the very place to which we should run in time of bereavement. There we are in touch with Jesus, and with all those who have gone before us with the sign of faith. The older we grow the more dear ones we ourselves have in heaven, the more real and concrete the place becomes for us. As we confess in the liturgy, "Therefore with angels and arch-angels and with all the company of heaven . . ." In Christ, they are all there. When St. Augustine lost his mother and his eight year old son, in his deep agony he made this beautiful statement: "He alone loses no dear one in whom all are dear in him who cannot be lost". Jesus, who is God, and who defeated death for us, cannot be lost. The gates of hell shall not prevail against him. It is he who is here. He is in touch with his Church. The Church is one. In him, all are there. He binds the Church together. This is the true consolation of Christians, whether we are separated by death or by continents. At the altar, we are still one. Because the Church is one body, be it in heaven or be it on earth, we are together. What we now believe, we shall then see.

Worship Services Must Reflect Faith

There are very deep dimensions here. Our worship services ought to reflect that this is what we believe. It reminds me of Solzhenitsyn. He said that when he was only a young child, he was taken to a church service —a Russian Orthodox service. The beauty of the singing, the obvious otherworldly emphasis on the heavenly reality of the resurrection, made such a deep impression on him, that no amount of personal suffering or intellectual argument later were able to wipe it out. I wonder how many of our children receive those impressions. They should! We are here dealing with the very realities of God. Our services ought to be a witness to this. This is a piece of heaven on earth.

Roman Catholics and the Sacrament

Today many conservative Roman Catholics are very distressed with liturgical reforms emanating from Vatican II. One incisive observer said. "There are more ways than one of changing doctrine. You can change doctrine just by what you practice, without ever changing the words." And that's what he alleged has happened since Vatican II with the Roman doctrine of the Real Presence. They have had trouble with liberals who, for example, in Holland have denied the Real Presence of Christ. A leading Roman theologian wished to substitute for the word transubstantiation, the word transignification. It prompted the sad joke some years ago about Holland, where liberal theologians were denying all sorts of things, including the Roman doctrine of transubstantiation: "In Holland everything changes, except bread and wine!" There is also a lot of Zwingliism creeping in in Rome. One of our Roman Catholic friends in Fort Wayne remembers what an atmosphere of awe it was, some years ago, when her sick father received the Sacrament. The priest came with candles and this tremendous mystery was transacted and brought to the sick. There was a public testimony. They believed this to be the true body of Christ. Later, her mother was in hospital and a female social worker came along and chitchatted about this and that. After her visit, she asked, "Would you like Communion?" She had a consecrated wafer in her handbag, which she was prepared to hand out. This devout woman said, "No, thank you!" She could not regard that as a Sacrament. There are many more ways of changing doctrine than one. How we behave with regard to the mysteries of God is a public confession of how important we think they are.

A Beautiful Communion Liturgy

I think that the liturgy that you have since Union in Australia is the best Lutheran liturgy in the English-speaking world. The music and the words are so fitting and so beautiful. In America, what has become very influential is a form of liturgy going back to the Anglican, Gregory Dix. He has popularized certain notions, which go back beyond him to some other scholars. According to him, the Sacrament is based on four actions: the Lord took bread, so since he took bread, we should have an offertory procession bringing the bread to the altar. Secondly, he broke it, so there must be a breaking of bread. Third, he gave thanks. Fourth, he distributed to them. So the taking — the offertory procession, the giving of thanks, of blessing, the breaking of bread, and the distribution to the communicants — this four-action scheme was uncritically, holus-bolus taken over by the intersynodical Lutheran Liturgical Commission and explicitly built into a new-fangled Lutheran Order of Service. It was most unfortunate. One Synod finally broke with that and went its own way, retaining the historic Common Service. The new liturgy is a kind of fussy ceremonialism. How decisive for the Sacrament is it to have an offertory procession? Is that really vital? Or why should one insist that one must have a particular kind of Eucharistic prayer? Or that you must have an act of breaking? Calvinists have always insisted that you must have this breaking. One King of Prussia was fanatically determined to compel the Lutherans in his kingdom to break the communion bread — which they refused to do — because the Calvinists demanded it. He was going to force them to do so by baking pieces of iron into the bread, compelling them to break it, unless they wanted to choke on it!

Consecration-Distribution-Reception

If the people on the Commission had read the Lutheran Confessions, they would have found in the *Formula of Concord* that if we are going to divide things into basic parts, we should start with the basic three in the *Formula of Concord*. There, the *Formula* goes to the heart of the matter:

what is essential to the Sacrament, what determines the sacramental action, are three things: consecration, distribution, reception. That's biblical. These are realities.

Emphasis on the Consecration

Luther laid great stress on the consecration because this is where the Word comes, and the Word finally makes everything. Without the Word of God, it is pure mumbo-jumbo. It was liturgically a very startling, radical innovation when, after hundreds of years, where the Words of Institution had been quietly mumbled at the altar so that nobody could hear, for the first time they were publicly chanted or spoken. There was a kind of bluntness or starkness about that. It was a public confession of what really is received in the Sacrament. Luther stressed the words of God which conveyed that.

Christ's Word Still Effective

The *Formula of Concord* says. "This is what makes the Sacrament, when Christ's words which he once spoke, are still effective whenever they are repeated". Christ, says Luther, has tied his action to our speaking. It's not anything we do. We could speak over bread for 1000 years and nothing would happen. But when Christ's Word is spoken, then it happens. The beautiful analogy of St. John Chrysostom is used. God said, **"Be fruitful and multiply!"** He said it only once, but that still works today in all the rich plant and animal life, including our life.

Christ once said, **"Do this in remembrance of me"**. Therefore, wherever this is done, these words are effective and produce what they say. Modern Lutherans are very dangerously forgetting the importance of the consecration. This is where the Word of Christ is attached to the element. That's what makes it a Sacrament. Then, of course, the rest has to follow. Luther would turn over in his grave if the Words of Institution were omitted, because for Luther the one thing that is necessary is the Word of Christ. That makes the Sacrament what it is.

Public Proclamation in the Sacrament

According to Article 24 of *The Apology*, which is a very rich statement concerning what we believe about the Sacrament, it is quite clear that one thing that is necessary is the public proclamation, so that you don't have a dumb rite going on — ritual without explanation. The sermon and the Sacrament belong together. Our forefathers, Luther and the Reformation theologians, always take the Pauline text, **1 Corinthians 11:26, "As often as you eat this bread and drink the cup, you proclaim the Lord's death until he comes",** as an indication that the Sacrament is to be celebrated in the context of proclamation. God's Word is there to be announced and then to be acted out and received in the Sacrament.

THE LUTHERAN, June 18, 1984
Christian News, October 15, 1984

1. The sacrament is primarily a ____.
2. Where is heaven? ____
3. What made a deep impression on Solzhenitsyn? ____
4. "In Holland everything changes except ____."
5. What determines the sacramental action? ____

HOW TO GIVE UP THE CONFESSIONS WITHOUT SEEMING TO

November 5, 1984

Bishop David Preus' article "Fellowship with other Christians," in ***The Lutheran Standard*** (20 January 1984), the official organ of the ALC, marks a major mile-stone in the history of Lutheranism in America. At least three lines of comment suggest themselves.

[1] *Scuttling the Minneapolis Theses*

Bishop Preus proposes changing what he calls "ALC policy regarding altar and pulpit fellowship." Specifically, he claims that the "results of bilateral dialogs with Reformed, Roman Catholic, and Episcopal Christians indicate that the ALC should, if those bodies agree, enter into altar and pulpit fellowship with them."

The enormous significance of this suggestion lies in the fact that the ALC's chief spokesman here publicly calls for the scuttling of his church's official position. That position was embodied in the ***Minneapolis Theses*** (1925), which served as the doctrinal foundation for both the (old) American Lutheran Church (1930) and the American Lutheran Conference (1930). Section III, on "Church Fellowship," in the ***Minneapolis Theses*** is so excellent, that it must be quoted in full:

1. These synods agree that true Christians are found in every denomination which has so much of divine truth revealed in Holy Scripture that children of God can be born in it; that according to the Word of God and our confessions, church fellowship, that is, mutual recognition, altar and pulpit fellowship, and eventually cooperation in the strictly essential work of the church, presupposes unanimity in the pure doctrine of the Gospel and of the confession of the same in word and deed. Where the establishment and maintenance of church fellowship ignores present doctrinal differences or declares them a matter of indifference, there is unionism, pretense of union which does not exist.
2. They agree that the rule, "Lutheran pulpits for Lutheran pastors only, and Lutheran altars for Lutheran communicants only," is not only in full accord with, but necessarily implied in, the teachings of the divine Word and the confessions of the evangelical Lutheran Church. This rule, implying the rejection of all unionism and syncretism must be observed as setting forth a principle elementary to sound and conservative Lutheranism.

The "new" ALC's Articles of Union (1958) reaffirmed the ***Minneapolis Theses*** of 1925, and also the ***United Testimony of Faith and Life*** of 1952. The ***United Testimony*** also specifically affirms that "Article III, Church Fellowship, ***Minneapolis Theses***,...furnishes the correct principles on fellowship for our Churches." But, adds the ***United Testimony***, "in the application of these principles, situations calling for exceptions will arise." This may seem to relativize the *Minneapolis Theses* to some extent. Nevertheless it is clear that what Presiding Bishop Preus is calling for is not simply more exceptions, but an abolition of the principles themselves.

It is interesting to note Fred W. Meuser's judgment that the *Minneapolis Theses*, on the one hand opposed "the suspicious and isolationist spirit of the Synodical Conference," but, on the other hand, "bore witness that on the issues of inspiration of the Scriptures, the Lutheran Confessions, fellowship with other churches, and attitude toward secret religious societies the U.L.C.A. was seriously deficient" (*The Formation of the American Lutheran Church,* 1958, pp. 247-248). Yet the *Minneapolis Theses* had, on the question of fellowship, taken their stand squarely on the "Galesburg Rule" (1875) formulated by the great Charles Porterfield Krauth for the General Council, a predecessor of the U.L.C.A. (now L.C.A.). This means that whatever differences existed in application, the traditional Lutheran fellowship principles were not a "Missourian" peculiarity, but were held in common by all the antecedent bodies of the ALC and by the General Council and the Augustana Synod components of the LCA. In abandoning this common Lutheran ground, today's merging bodies are deliberately taking their stand far below the level even of the old, confessionally flabby General Synod!

[2] *Churches or "Other Christians"?*

That tell-tale word "policy" in the very first sentence already suggests that the whole matter of church fellowship lies in the plane not of basic doctrine, but of practical action, hence "policy." This is probably inevitable if one thinks of fellowship as having to do with individuals rather than with churches as such. And that is clearly the case in this article. The very heading proclaims that the issue is perceived to be one of fellowship with "other Christians," rather than with churches. Churches are mentioned, to be sure, but the over-riding category is that of "Christians," that is, individuals. That notion, in turn, is no doubt heavily colored in terms of actual people one has met, or, in Bishop Preus' own words, "personal enrichment through shared experiences with non-Lutheran Christians" and "deepening fellowship experiences." If fellowship is seen only or mainly under the aspect of individuals, perhaps of persons near and dear, and if churches are seen basically as aggregates of such individuals, then charity will of course dictate a "policy" of broad inclusiveness.

This person-centered approach is by no means unusual. It is in fact the prevailing view of things, which we take in with the very air we breathe. Contemporary culture, disseminated by the mass media, knows nothing beyond the immediacies of individual human existence, understood largely in biological terms. Knowing no history, democratic mass culture cannot sustain the mental effort to think trans-personally, in terms of great historical movements or long-term strategic relationships. It is easier to gush about individual people and their hopes and fears, to assume that everyone in the world is basically "just like the folks next door," and to project Madison Avenue fantasy worlds, in which peace and survival depend not so much on tough-minded strategic realism as on the magic of personal feelings and relations. (Hence the cosmic significance, on silly celluloid, of CIA-KGB love affairs!) We have here that "preoccupation with the self and its experiences, promoted by and promoting the subjectivist analysis of moral, aesthetic, metaphysical and theological judgments" which C.E.M. Joad has so well placed among the "stigmata of decadence." Given this sort of cultural mood or climate, churches are soon following suit. The Missouri Synod's own CTCR produced in the early sixties a rather wobbly sort of "Theology of Fellowship." Henry P. Hamann wrote of it in the Australian sister church's official critique:

> The tendency throughout — and it is intentional — is not to speak of churches, but to speak of individuals. For with them, in accordance with the subjective **proton pseudos** at the basis of the whole presentation, we can — at least so it is held — distinguish those who are plainly not of Christ...and those who are true Christians.... Surely one must see that the true counterpart in our day to the false teachers of the New Testament age are the heterodox church-bodies themselves.

Now, the great confessions of our church also know and speak of Christian individuals — but how differently! The church, as a seven-year-old child praying the Creed knows, is "holy believers and sheep who hear the voice of their Shepherd" (SA.III:XII). The holy believers and sheep, whom only God knows as such, are accessible to us only indirectly, through the voice of their Shepherd, in the purely proclaimed Gospel and the rightly administered Sacraments. Even the much maligned Formula of Concord is at pains to aim its doctrinal condemnations at *false systems, not their victims as such, viz.,* "those persons who err ingenuously and who do not blaspheme the truth of the divine Word, and far less do we mean entire churches...." (Preface) But the presence of captive Israel in Babylon is not allowed to soften or blunt faithful resistance to the latter. The Formula does not hesitate to say that the Augsburg Confession "distinguishes our reformed churches from the papacy and from other condemned sects and heresies" (FC SD, Rule and Norm, 5)!

Here lies the theological greatness of Luther's "ecclesiology of the cross" (just the point of Augsburg Confession VII!). This understanding of the church is broad enough to include every single child of God and narrow enough to exclude every denial of the uniquely saving Gospel and Sacraments.

The whole church is bound up with the whole Gospel—one Lord, one Faith, one Baptism! This ecumenical perspective is truly evangelical because it pays attention only to the saving gift of God, not to the impressive vanities of "religious man." It therefore liberates one from being "blown here and there by every wind of teaching and by the cunning and craftiness of men in their deceitful scheming" (Eph. 4:14 NIV). This is precisely where Luther and the modern ecumenical movement part company. Both confess one single universal church — but where Luther walks humbly, by faith, the ecumenical movement insists on sight. For him the starting point is the Gospel, the *known,* which alone determines the value of the unknown in the "ecumenical equation," the church. The ecumenical movement does the opposite. Its starting point, or the known, is the visible, institutional church organization, or rather the aggregate of such organizations. The Gospel is the unknown, the "X," which must be calculated from the institutional givens — that is, where at least two or three hundred million are gathered together. This is "theology of glory" with a vengeance!

For Luther the church is part and parcel of the Christ mystery and, as such, totally inaccessible to all human wisdom. Humbly "hidden under the cross" in this age (Ap, VII-VIII,18), the church is to be found and grasped only in the holy Gospel and Sacraments of Christ, but there fully. Uplifting encounters with "other Christians" are no substitute for the one holy church known and recognized by faith alone, in her pure marks alone. Based on, and limited by, these marks, church fellowship does not depend on our subjective guesses about just how far afield "other Christians" might still be found.

[3] *Confession versus Church Politics*

Contrary to the Gospel as understood in the Book of Concord, the ALC's Presiding Bishop Preus urges full church fellowship with both the Roman and the Reformed churches. He cites in support the results of "bilateral dialogs." How vacuous these results are is clear from Bishop Preus' own admission that "debate with the Reformed churches as to the mode of Christ's real presence in the sacrament can continue without separation at altar and pulpit." But of course it is totally false to suggest that the Lutheran and Reformed churches agree on Christ's real presence but differently about the "mode." No Zwinglian or Calvinist has ever denied that Christ, the Person, is "really present" in His divine nature, not only in the Sacrament, but at any meal at all, and indeed everywhere. What the Reformed churches have denied, and continue to deny, is that the Savior distributes His real body and blood under the consecrated bread and wine, so that all communicants receive these, and not simply "by faith," but bodily, with the mouth. That, and not a vague, Calvinistic "real presence of Christ," is the clear and unanimous sacramental teaching of our Confessions, from the Catechisms and the Augsburg Confession to the Smalcald Articles and the Formula of Concord. Current diplomatic compromises and evasions about the Sacrament of the Altar are meant to allow just the sort of positions which "cannot be tolerated in the church of God, much less be excused and defended," according to the Formula of Concord (SD, Rule and Norm, 9).

As for the Roman-Lutheran dialogue in the U.S.A., the lengthy justification document is impressive in some ways, but finally signals an impasse at best or a Lutheran surrender at worst. For while the Roman Catholic party retreats not one inch from the Council of Trent,* the Lutherans, with some assistance from the Lutheran World Federation, are torn between the Bible and their Confessions on the one hand, and historical criticism on the other. In the end the Lutherans yield to the traditional Roman confusion between justification and internal renewal or transformation (par. 156-5)! Yet this is the very article by which the church either stands or falls, and of which our church confesses with Luther in the Smalcald Articles: "Nothing in this article can be given up or compromised, even if heaven and earth and things temporal should be destroyed" (SA, II,1.5). And now full church fellowship is urged on the basis of what is admittedly "not fully equivalent to the Reformation teaching on justification" (par. 157).

Bishop Preus is of course aware that all is not well: "We continue to have significant theological and organizational differences with such bodies." But he thinks that the difficulty can be met:

> Hence, it is important that Lutherans and others maintain their existence within their confessional bodies. The differences are significant enough that confessional identities should be acknowledged, but the differences are not significant enough to keep us from expressing our unity at the altar and in the pulpit.

This proposal, however, really makes matters worse. It amounts to the Lutheran World Federation's notion of "Reconciled Diversity," which expressly combines "genuine church fellowship" with "the legitimacy of the confessional differences and therefore the need to preserve them" (LWF 1977, **Proceedings,** p. 174). The LWF has here radicalized the approach of the Prussian Union (Lutheran and Reformed) of the last century: each church can keep its confession, but the differences are no longer regarded as church-divisive. The Church of the Augsburg Confession is downgraded to one school of thought among others, within a broad communion in which many confessions have equal rights.

To think that one can preserve "confessional identities" while granting church fellowship to contrary confessions is pure illusion. If the confessions are not allowed to define the boundaries of church fellowship, then they have been set aside as confessions. To yield the theological substance of church fellowship while withholding organizational trifles is sectarian. It preserves nothing more than "bureaucratic identities." So called "confessions" which are not confessed in pulpits and at altars are play confessions. To rely instead on some sort of institutional, organizational pressure, is to put church politics in the place of theology. And this stands Augsburg Confession VII precisely on its head: the one thing needful, agreement in the pure Gospel and Sacraments ("in the doctrine and in all its articles," FC SD X, 31) is given up to promiscuous altar and pulpit fellowship, while the "human traditions", which are "not necessary" are, in the form of bureaucratic structures, relied on to project pseudoconfessional "identities."

How do Lutheran churches respond today to such public abandonment of their confessions? It remains to be seen. One can agree, in one sense, with Presiding Bishop Preus: "These matters must be discussed and debated in the church. Bring out your best biblical thinking. Do not be intimidated by anyone who sounds like [sic] he or she has all the answers." But those who have in Confirmation confessed the Faith of the Small Catechism, and especially those who have, in Ordination, sworn a solemn oath to teach in accordance with the Book of Concord, should have *some* answers.

Concordia Theological Observer
Christian News, November 5, 1984

* When the *Christian News* editor visited the church in Augsburg, Germany where the Joint Roman Catholic-Lutheran Declaration on Justification was signed, a Roman Catholic theologian, who had come from Rome, told the editor that despite the joint statement, Rome still affirmed the Canons and Decrees of Trent, which in Session VI Canon 12 says:

"If anyone saith that justifying faith is nothing else but confidence in the divine mercy which remits sins for Christ's sake; or that this confidence alone is that whereby we are justified; let him be anathema."

A card distributed at some Roman Catholic funerals in the U.S. in 2015 has a painting of the Virgin Mary on one side. On the back is this statement "In loving Memory of" the deceased Roman Catholic.

"O gentlest Heart of Jesus, ever present in the Blessed Sacrament, ever consumed with burning love for the poor captive souls in Purgatory, have mercy on the soul of Thy departed servant.

"Be not severe in Thy Judgment, but let some drops of Thy precious blood fall upon the devouring flames, and do Thou, O Merciful Savior, send Thy angels to conduct thy departed servant to a place of refreshment, light and peace.
Amen"

1. ALC Bishop David Preus suggested ____ the Minneapolis Theses.
2. The Minneapolis Theses said ____ pulpits for ____ only and Lutheran Altars for ____ only.
3. Who formulated the "Galesburg Rule?" ____
4. The Missouri Synod's CTCR in the early sixties produced a rather wobbly ____.
5. A seven year old child praying the creed knows that the church is ____.
6. Where do Luther and the modern ecumenical movement part company? ____
7. The Roman Catholic justification document signals ____.
8. Did Rome retreat from the Council of Trent? ____

THE LORD'S SUPPER

November 5, 1984

The Lord's Supper is often simply called The Sacrament. When Luther spoke of The Sacrament, he meant this Sacrament although, of course, Baptism is just as much a Sacrament. But this has a kind of pre-eminence. While Baptism is something you do only once, the Lord's Supper is done repeatedly. It becomes the constant experience of the Christian. When you think of it, in this Sacrament all basic lines of Christian truth come together.

The Sacrament Is The Gospel

It is sad to see that Christendom is divided on this Sacrament of love. People say — especially those who want to point their finger at the Church. "Isn't it ironic? The Lord gave a feast of love and this feast of love becomes a bone of contention. Isn't there something wrong when people debate about the very thing which is supposed to create unity in the Church?" But it cannot be otherwise, because in the Sacrament all lines of Christian truth converge. Whatever one says about any part of Christian truth will have an effect on the Sacrament. Luther is able to say simply, **The Sacrament is the Gospel**. Mind you, he didn't say, the Gospel is the Sacrament. But he did say the Sacrament is the Gospel.

The Lines Come Together

Notice the lines that come together! Take, for instance, the doctrine of the atonement. What could be more important in Christian truth than the doctrine of atonement? It is the very heart of the Sacrament, because it is the blood of the New Covenant shed for you. The atonement is involved — with the cross at the center.

When it comes to Christology, there is immediately debate. How can Christ be here? How are his humanity and his divinity related? You can't avoid the question of the nature of the person and work of Jesus Christ — the very heart of the faith. Nor can you avoid the question of authority in the Church, the question of the nature of biblical truth and apostolic authority. St. Paul writes, **"I received from the Lord what I also delivered to you, that the Lord Jesus, on the night when he was betrayed, took bread..."** In other words, you have to decide what is the authority of this text. All the important issues converge in the Sacrament. This is where the whole Gospel comes to a head.

A Sacrifice of Thanksgiving

What troubled Luther at the time of the Reformation was the idea that the body and blood of Christ were sacrificed anew by the priest as a true, but unbloody sacrifice, that is, as a propitiatory sacrifice which really took away sin, and therefore which had to be regarded either as a kind of repetition or as a completion of Calvary. Luther saw that this really attacks the sufficiency of the one sacrifice of Christ. The idea horrified him. He realized that it was basically a misinterpretation, a misunderstanding of the language about sacrifice. The Early Church did not teach that the body and blood of Christ were sacrificed, but that we sacrifice ourselves in thanksgiving, in response to what God has given us. Luther came to see very clearly that the basic direction of the Sacrament is not something from us to God, from down here to up there. The basic direction of the Sacrament is God's gift to us. The arrow goes from heaven to earth — not from earth to heaven.

The Sacrament As Pure Gift

If we take the traditional division of elements in worship into sacramental and sacrificial, sacramental is what God does to us, and sacrificial is our response which we offer to him. The Sacrament belongs entirely in the former area. The body and blood of Christ are given us in the Sacrament, not that we might offer them to God; he is offering them to us. This is what Luther understood very clearly and what he maintained with absolute and total integrity. This is why he took the Canon of the Mass, which to him looked like one of those stranded vessels near Caloundra, in Queensland, which accumulated barnacles over the years. These barnacles obscured the original meaning of the thing itself. Luther threw out all this sacrifice language which gave a false impression, and restored to the Church this marvelous understanding of the Sacrament as pure gift — not as a requirement or a performance — but as pure gift from God, not needing any human completion. That was quite a radical development, and a radical restoration of the whole notion of what the Gospel means.

In the Middle Ages the distinction between Law and Gospel had been very much obscured. If Luther is able to say that the Sacrament is the Gospel, that's not just a little slogan. He means that the Sacrament is Gospel, not Law. It is fundamentally gift, not requirement. There are two entirely opposite doctrines in the Bible. The Law tells us what to do. It requires something of us, and judges us and the very thing which people depend on so much. You may hear that at funerals, too. "He was such a good man. He surely went to heaven. Look how good he was!" As if our goodness, measured by our keeping of the Law, is the thing that can possibly get us into the grace of God! No, that's a response! The real thing, the primary thing is that God gives us everything in his Son, No strings attached, nothing required!

The Alien Work of God

Taking an obscure text in Isaiah, Luther speaks of the two works of God as the alien, or strange work of God, and the proper work of God. What is this strange work of God? The strange work of God is to terrify and to judge. He does that by the Law. There we meet the anger of God. We cannot pretty that up and make it sugary and pleasant. Unless we face up to the fact of the anger of God and to the radicalness of our evil, we shall never appreciate the Gospel or take it seriously. So the alien, the strange work of God, is this, that he terrifies through the Law and brings us down to size, so that we know we are dust and ashes before him.

The Proper Work of God

But that is not his real work. His proper work is to comfort, to console, to lift up. If he kills, it's only in order to make alive. It's like old-fashioned hunting. I have never participated very much in modern hunting. But in old-fashioned hunting I believe that the hunters divided into two groups. One lot of hunters would make a frightful din to frighten the game and chase them in the direction of the others, who would then shoot them or neatly capture them.

So God has this two-fold operation. He makes a frightful din with the Law, to frighten us for a purpose, in order to drive us into the saving net of the Gospel so that we may be caught for our own good — not for his benefit; he doesn't get anything out of it — so that we might be transferred from darkness to light, from the kingdom of death to the kingdom of life. Luther understood that this great gift, where the body and the blood — the very elements which secured our salvation — are distributed, is pure Gospel. That is the most proper work of God. Here we have a window opened directly into the heart of God. If we want to know what God is really like, what his real intention to us is, as penitent sinners, then we must hear these words: **"Take, eat, this is my body, given for you"**.

Two Kinds of Sacrifice

But is there anything sacrificial there at all? St. Paul would say, "Yes, very much, in every way". But we need to see that there are two kinds of sacrifice —propitiatory and eucharistic. The propitiatory sacrifice is one which actually secures remission of sins, which pays for sin, which secures mercy in place of wrath. *Eucharistic* comes from a Greek word which means a sacrifice of praise and thanksgiving. For Martin Chemnitz, who was a great student of Luther, the favorite name of the Sacrament was Eucharist, because this great sacrifice from God is received by us with thanksgiving,

The Sacrifice of Christ

There is only one kind of propitiatory sacrifice. All sacrifices you could name have to be either propitiatory or eucharistic. No third type exists. Among the propitiatory, there is only one: the sacrifice of Christ. Not even the Old Testament sacrifice of the blood of bulls and goats in itself took away sin. It worked like a credit card. It's not the plastic that matters. It works because somebody is willing to accept it, because later full payment will be made.

The Old Testament sacrifices were symbolic sacrifices. They really worked because of the power of God. But the credit which the Old Testament sacrifices gave out was to be paid for when the Lamb of God carried all the sins of the world and made good for them on the cross. There is only one truly propitiatory sacrifice and that is the sacrifice of Christ. That's what Luther insisted on. We cannot mix and mingle anything else into this one sacrifice which was complete when Christ said, "It is finished". It was accomplished, and no man could add to the completed work of Christ. The whole act of salvation for mankind is there. That means the table, the dinner, is set for all of us. If anybody starves, he is starving in the face of plenty, not because there isn't enough. The plate is actually filled. The sacrifice is there. No one need miss out.

Eucharistic Sacrifices

All other sacrifices are eucharistic. In connection with the Sacrament, there are eucharistic elements. Even in ordinary life, it is simply bad manners to receive anything without giving thanks. How much more when we receive the greatest gift of all, the greatest gift on earth, when God gives us his Son in the immediacy and directness of the Real Presence of the Eucharist, can we fail to say "thank you" to him as we receive it! This great gift is surrounded by eucharistic sacrifices: the giving of thanks, praising, adoring God, receiving all from him. This is the context, too, in which our offerings should be seen. Everything in the service that praises God should be seen as a response. It is very bad if we see the Sacrament — as it is often seen — as a kind of afterthought, which is God's response to our previous efforts. It's the other way around! All our offerings, all our thanksgivings, are in response to God's great gift. All the sacrifices we offer are small and very humble compared to the great sacrifice that God has given to us.

This is captured in Acts 2:42 — the other text I wanted to refer to, where it says of the Early Church that they continued steadfastly, that is, faithfully, consistently, with integrity, without interruption in four things: **"the Apostles' teaching, fellowship, breaking of bread, and the prayers."** These four are a unit. They belong together,

Sharing the Gospel

I want to talk about that second word *fellowship,* the Greek *koinonia.* When we today speak of fellowship, it often has a vague ring. Fellowship could be a kind of feeling, or an experience, or a mood. The New Testament didn't mean anything vague like that. Dr. Sasse and others hold that when the New Testament uses the word *fellowship* in these contexts, it means something very concrete. It means the mutual care that we show, specifically also by our offerings. Our offerings become a concrete expression of that. This is what Paul means when he says you have a share with me, you are participants with me, in the Gospel. You are supporting it with your substance. Offerings need to be regarded by the Church, and by us as Christians, not as something left over. "The Church has a budget, so we obviously have to do something." It is part of our "spiritual worship" — not only the money that I give to the Church, but also the money that I use to buy my wife a new frock when she needs it — which isn't all that often! — shoes for my children, books, anything like that. It's silly to say, "We spent all this on ourselves and this on God".

No! We should see to it that everything we spend is for God. We are to spend for God everything we are and have and do. Some of it has to go to the Church, some of it has to go for this and some for that — but all of it is for God. The care for other people and for those whom we know to be in need among our relatives and friends —this is also a very important thing in the sight of God.

Taking Christ's Words at Face Value

The second great dispute at the time of the Reformation centered on what was really given in the Sacrament. There were some, notably Zwingli and others, who said, "Well, it isn't really the body of Christ. It's only a picture. It's like a flag. It's a symbol, but it isn't the real thing."

Luther began an enormously productive work in defending the realistic understanding, which fundamentally is the only honest understanding, of the text. You can't really imagine the Lord, on the most solemn night of his life, saying something that he didn't quite mean, or meaning something that he didn't quite say. He uses the careful legal language of a last will and testament. In a testament you don't leave pictures unless they are by somebody like Namatjira, or which have value in themselves. The language in a testament, in a legal document, is to be construed literally. It's not a parable. It's not a vision such as you have in the *Book of Revelation* or *Daniel* which is clearly a language of a vision or a dream that should not be pressed literally, it even says it's a vision. But when it says it's not a vision, but the last will and testament of the Son of God on the last night of his life on earth — that, for some reason, is not to be taken literally, as Zwingli and some others stated.

I don't understand this strange inconsistency. This is very solemn, legal language. Therefore, when Jesus says, **"This is my body"**, no man has the right to interpret that to mean "This is not my body". When he says it is his body, we have to take that at face value. Lest there be any doubt about the words themselves, St. Paul makes it quite clear what is meant when in 1 Corinthians 10:16, for example, he says, **"The cup of blessing which we bless, is it not a participation in the blood of Christ? The bread which we break, is it not a participation in the body of Christ?"** In the next chapter he warns against unworthy reception of this mystery and says, If you receive it unworthily, that is improperly, disrespectfully, you are guilty of dishonoring not symbols, but the Lord's body and blood!

The Sacrament - The Life of The Church

Even very liberal theologians, who believe all of this is so much myth and legend, say quite honestly: Yes, Paul meant that the body and blood of Christ are really given in the Sacrament. That's the only honest way of understanding these words. Luther was infuriated when people danced around the obvious meaning of the text and refused to submit to the Word as it read. For Luther that wasn't just a matter of being right in principle. The Germans have a beautiful word, *Rechthaberei,* which means "given to disputation", "specializing in being right". Luther wasn't interested in that. For him the Sacrament was the life of the Church, and it was his own life. He was prepared to be killed rather than have the Church robbed of this great treasure, which he identified with the Gospel itself. In 1529, at Marburg in Germany, Luther and Zwingli got together and debated this thing. It's deeply moving to read the report of that debate. The late great German-Australian theologian, Dr. Hermann Sasse, has done us all a favor by giving us that in English, in the appendix of his book, *This Is My Body*. If you are at all interested in a deeper study of this background, do read this book. It has been a great eye-opener for many pastors and theologians, and has made confessing ministers of the Word of many people.

The Wittenberg "Concord" Disavowed

By the time the *Augsburg Confession* was presented in 1530, there were already two parties to the Reformation, which could not be brought to a common denominator. All efforts failed until 1536, after a lot of bitterness and debate back and forth. In 1536 a remarkable thing happened. Representing, as everybody thought, the southern churches and also the Swiss, delegates came to Wittenberg and worked out an agreement with Luther, Melanchthon and the Wittenberg theologians, signed the *Wittenberg Concord* of 1536, and clearly confessed the true presence of Christ's body and blood in the Sacrament. It seemed a miracle. Luther was very happy. He often seemed a rough man, but when there was agreement in the faith, he was deeply moved. There was a joint Communion Service. They embraced each other in the fellowship of the one faith. Everybody celebrated the fact that the rift seemed to have been healed. But then the agreement was disavowed and discredited. People found loopholes in it. Finally, the thing fell apart. The Concord didn't hold. Luther was deeply disappointed, and felt that he had been misled and cheated.

Truly Present In the Sacrament

We believe that Jesus Christ is truly present in the Sacrament. But suppose somebody says only that, Jesus is truly present at every Christian breakfast isn't he? We pray: "Come, Lord Jesus, be our guest; let these thy gifts to us be blest". Jesus is really there. But that's not a Sacrament. Jesus is present with the bread and wine in Holy Communion in a way in which he is not simply a normal table guest. It is not enough to say that Jesus is there. The point is, do we believe what he says, that with the bread, he gives us his body; with the wine, he gives us his blood?

Others suggest that Jesus Christ is there, but that he is there only by faith. He is not really there. However, our faith doesn't make any of God's blessings. Our faith only receives what is there. Luther is being very true to the New Testament when he says all the things of God must be there before faith can receive them. Faith doesn't create anything. It only receives what is already there. If there is nothing there, faith has nothing to receive. With the bread, which the mouth receives, we receive the body of God into our very bodies. Unworthy communicants also receive the true body and blood of the Savior. If one doesn't say that, one doesn't really teach the Real Presence.

A Farfetched Interpretation

Calvin tried to say, "Yes, I believe that the body and blood of Christ are really there". He explained it like this: "The body of Christ is really far away, out there in heaven somewhere. But the Holy Spirit is here with us. He bridges the gap between the absent body of Christ and me. So in that sense we have some connection with the body of Christ." But a moment's thought will show how far-fetched and fundamentally, intellectually dishonest that is. By the same token we could say that we have St Peter present in the Sacrament, because the Holy Spirit is also in touch with St Peter somewhere, and with St Paul and the Blessed Virgin.

This is not a serious interpretation of the words. A serious interpretation must take seriously that Jesus gives his body and blood, and that the unworthy communicant is warned lest he be guilty of dishonoring the body and blood of Christ. Our *Confessions* make the interesting point that this could not be referring to spiritual participation in Christ, because nobody should be warned against spiritual participation in Christ. Nobody can do any damage by spiritually eating and drinking of Christ. Only if we take the sacramental body and blood of Christ unworthily, are we guilty of the body and blood of Christ. St Paul is not talking about a spiritual participation, which can never be wrong; he is speaking of an outward participation, a sacramental participation, which will do damage if we receive it unworthily. Everything hinges on this reality,

Given From the Altar

The **propitiatory** sacrifice of Christ is given us from the altar. That body and that blood of Christ which are the sacrifice which won our salvation, are now being returned to us by God. I think the best way to look at it is from the analogy of the Old Testament sacrifices. Supposing that your family were to sacrifice in the temple — how would that work? You would bring an animal. The animal would be killed and given to the priest. The priest would divide the meat into three parts. One part would be sacrificed to God. One part would be given to the priests for their sustenance. And one part would be given back to the family. You would then gather around and have a sacrificial meal. You would eat that meat as a token, and as a way of participating in the sacrifice, by which you show that this is your sacrifice that is being offered, and also that this has been returned to you as a guarantee that God is giving you the blessing which is meted out to your sacrifice. So there would be these three parts: one to God, one to the priests, and one given back to the people.

The Whole, Completed Sacrifice

In the New Testament it is quite different. The entire sacrifice, Christ himself, is given to God. Do you recall the beautiful Eucharistic hymn. *Himself the victim, and himself the* priest? This entire sacrifice is offered to God. He doesn't give back to us in the Eucharist merely a third. He gives back to us **the whole, completed sacrifice**. The sacrifice has done its work. Now God returns, not a third, but all of it as a family of God, gathered at the altar of God, we receive back this fullness, this wholeness of God in Christ, as our sacramental banquet. And what does he want in response? In response, he wants from us not one-third or one-tenth or tithe. Some people make a superstitious fuss about ten percent. I once saw a sign in front of a church: "One day in seven belongs to heaven." That is quite a wrong ratio, because every day in seven belongs to heaven. We baptized Christians are full-time priests of God. What does a priest do? The basic business of priests is to sacrifice. We are baptized priests of God. That some of us happen to be ministers is not very important. The important thing is that we are all baptized priests who offer Eucharistic sacrifices — praise and thanksgiving. As Peter said: we are to "declare the wonderful deeds of him who called you out of darkness into his marvelous light". That's our priestly work.

"Your Bodies A Living Sacrifice"
I'd like to draw your attention to two texts. One is Romans 12:1, where Paul writes: "I appeal to you therefore, brethren, by the mercies of God, to present your bodies as a living sacrifice, holy and acceptable to God, which is your spiritual worship". Let me say it once again: God has received the entire sacrifice. This has made peace between God and man. He now gives back the entire sacrifice to us in the Eucharist. We cannot speak of bits and pieces in that context. That would be sacrilege. This is the whole Christ, given to us with his body and blood. In response, he asks that we give him all of ourselves. "I appeal to you by the mercies — the propitiatory sacrifice — of God, to present your bodies". Note the emphasis on body! Wouldn't it sound more religious to say your souls or yourselves? No, that would be too airy-fairy. It's much more concrete when he says, "present your bodies". It's much too easy to sacrifice your soul. You can think you're sacrificing your soul, while the body snores on in lazy smugness. Therefore Paul says, "present your bodies". If the body is involved, then we know we are involved. If it's only the soul, that could be something mental. That is too easy, too simple. The whole life of the Christian is a priestly service in response to the great self-giving of God.

The Lutheran (Australia)
Christian News, November 5, 1984

1. All basic lines of Christian truth come together in ____.
2. Luther said "The Sacrament is the ____."
3. The basic direction of the Sacrament is ____.
4. What is the only propitiatory sacrifice? ____
5. We should see to it that everything we spend is for ____.
6. Do unworthy communicants receive the body and blood of the Savior?____
7. Christ gives back to us ____.
8. Every day belongs to ____.
9. What is our priestly work? ____

UNREAL LANGUAGE ABOUT THE REAL PRESENCE

November 5, 1984

Until now the words "real presence" have been a veritable test phrase for the Biblical. Lutheran doctrine that in the Holy Supper the Lord gives His real, actual body and blood to all communicants. Thanks to the new, highly inflationary ecumenical currency, the term "real presence" has lost most of its value. The Lutheran-Reformed Dialogue, Series 111 (1981-1983), dares to allege, not that Lutheran and Reformed churches have now at last found agreement in this matter, but that both churches have always "strongly affirmed the real presence of Christ in the Sacrament" *(An Invitation to Action,* p. 16). The differences are said to be only over the mode or manner of this presence, and therefore are really not divisive. If bankers took such liberties with the temporal treasures entrusted to them, they would end up with long prison terms.

That Christ is personally present not only in the Sacrament but in every Christian gathering, and indeed everywhere, has never been in dispute between Lutherans and Reformed. What the Calvinists have always denied, and continue to deny, is that the Lord does something in the Sacrament which He does nowhere else, namely, feeds His communicants with His very body and blood, "in, with, and under" the consecrated bread and wine. This, and only this, is the clear teaching of the Lutheran Confessions. Those who have sworn a solemn oath to teach and practice in accordance with the Book of Concord, cannot advocate the position of Lutheran-Reformed Dialogue III without committing perjury.

It remains to be seen whether the ALC, the LCA, and the AELC, fully preoccupied with their merger, will accept the recommendations of their dialogue representatives.If so, the "New Lutheran Church" will have built into its very foundations a sell-out of the Sacrament.

If this tragedy and travesty, takes place, then only because the old Lutheran consciousness of the sacramental presence has receded into the background in the piety of many modern Lutherans. The awful surrenders now taking place before our very eyes, and quite painlessly, it seems, ought to shake would-be confessional Lutheran churches out of all smugness and complacency.

Since the proper catechism training is vital here, the question must always be asked, to what extent contemporary explanations actually do justice to the Book of Concord. It is interesting to compare here three conservative Lutheran expositions of the Catechism:

(A) the 1943 "Missouri" or "Blue" Catechism;

(B) the 1981 "ELS" (Evangelical Lutheran Synod) Catechism;

(C) the 1982 "Wisconsin" (Wisconsin Evangelical Lutheran Synod) Catechism.

(A): *299. What does Christ give us in, with, and under these visible means in the Lord's Supper?*

In, with, and under the *bread* Christ gives us His *true body;* in with, and under the *wine* He gives us His *true blood.* (Real Presence).

(B): *306. What does Jesus give us in the Sacrament under the earthly elements of bread, and wine?*

Under the earthly elements of bread and wine Jesus gives us His true body and blood which he delivered up for us on the cross for the forgiveness of our sins.

309. Are the bread and wine changed into the body and blood of Jesus?

In the Sacrament the bread and wine are not, changed into the body and blood of Christ, but are so intimately united with them that He can say that the bread and wine are His body and blood.

(C): *287. What does Jesus tell us is present together with the bread and wine in Holy Communion!*

Jesus tells us that His real body is present with the bread and that His real blood is present with the wine. (Real presence).

288. What do we receive, therefore, together with the bread and the wine in Holy Communion!

In Holy Communion we receive the true body of Christ together with the bread and the true blood of Christ together with the wine.

(A) here is adequate in light of the explanation of "under, with, and in" in Formula of Concord (SD), VII, (35-40).

(B) is even stronger, reflecting in Question 306 the "under" of Augsburg Confession X, and in Question, 309 the Smalcald Articles' confession that "the bread and the wine in the Supper are the true body and blood of Christ."

(C) is clearly the weakest of the three. Of the three prepositions, "in, with, and under," the word "with" stands for the loosest connection. It is no accident therefore that the Altered Augsburg Confession of 1540 used "with" by itself, and that this became a popular way to make Calvinistic teaching sound Lutheran. The weaselly-worded Leuenberg Agreement (1973) between Lutheran, Reformed, and Union churches, says that "the risen Jesus Christ imparts himself in his body and blood, given up for all, through his word of promise with bread and wine." A recent LCUSA Immigration and Refugee Service booklet for Laotians, *What Christians Believe,* drops "body and blood" completely, and teaches a weak form of Calvinism: "As Christians we believe that in the Lord's Supper Jesus Christ is truly present to assure us of forgiveness and to give us life and salvation."

None of these denials are of course intended in or countenanced by "C". Yet stronger language is needed if the full Biblical confession of the Book of Concord is to be transmitted to the next generation, given our "anything-goes" climate. "C", incidentally, does give the formula "in, with, and under," but only in an ambiguous diagram in which "our pastor gives us bread and wine" while "Christ gives us his body and blood" (p. 255). How foreign such a separation was to our forefathers is clear from a report in the Missouri Synod's official organ *Der Lutheraner,* (Vol. 14. No. 11, p. 84), of a Free Conference held in Pittsburgh, PA, in 1857. The Conference, with 48 participants, 22 of them "Missourians," having read Article X of the Augsburg Confession, found that there was no need for further discussion since all were agreed that the Lord's body and blood in the Sacrament were present "as well in the hands of the administrant, as in the mouth of the communicants"!

AFFIRM, October, 1984
Christian News, November 5, 1984

1. The Calvinists have always denied and continue to deny ____.
2. What has happened to the old Lutheran consciousness of the sacramental presence? ____

TURBULENCE AND DIVISION

November 19, 1984

In the Lutheran Churches of America, we have a lot of turbulence at the moment. Several Synods are uniting and some have divided. There is an air of instability and insecurity, and a lot of propaganda. Some say, "If you agree on the Gospel, then Churches should unite". What does it mean to agree on the Gospel? Some would answer: "Jesus died for you. We are agreed on the Gospel." But that doesn't begin to do justice to what is involved here. For our Lutheran confessors, the Gospel is not one little article in the Augsburg Confession which must be accepted and all the others can be surrendered. The heart of the Gospel — the doctrine of justification — is an article which illuminates all the others, but it doesn't eliminate them. Modern Lutherans tend to make of the **Article of Justification** a kind of principle with which they can eliminate all the rest. But that's not so. In the Confessions, in the Book of Concord, the full Gospel is what the Church confesses — not some mini-Gospel, some little slogan which you can easily say and not really be agreed on.

Essence of Church Fellowship

Take the question of Close Communion! This touches very much on the very definition of church fellowship. Church fellowship is not simply what you and I do as individuals. Nor does it concern the lovely people we meet here and there, with whom we could study the Bible together, with whom we can have a good conversation, with whom we can even pray together. That isn't church fellowship. **The essence of church fellowship is where the public administration of the means of grace is involved.** Church fellowship isn't something that private individuals do as such. Church fellowship is where decisions are made, at which altar and at which pulpit we belong. That has to do with **the public marks of the Church.**

The Most Public Confession

We need to see that the Sacrament of the Altar is never a purely private exercise. There is no such thing, strictly speaking, as private Communion. St. Paul says it beautifully in 1 Corinthians 10. *"We who are many are one body, for we all partake of the one bread."* Melanchthon tended to emphasize the Sacraments as activities. Luther emphasized what the thing is, in and of itself by God's Word. Dr. Sasse said: "It is not our action of the Eucharist that makes us one. It is the content of the cup. It is the Lord's body and his blood — not our doing something about it. These are the great realities which make us one." Therefore, the Lord's Supper is always a public, in fact, **the** most public confession of the Church. The Church can do nothing more official than celebrate the Holy Eucharist.

The Eucharist - A Culmination

Our forefathers always pointed to 1 Corinthians 11:26, *"As often as you eat this bread and drink the cup, you proclaim the Lord's death until he comes".* To receive the Sacrament is to make a public confession. It isn't simply believing one isolated doctrine — that the body and blood of Christ are really there. The confession of the Eucharist is that we are one, that I believe that the doctrine taught at the altar is the pure Gospel, and the Sacraments are as Christ gave them. This is why the Eucharist is a sort of culmination, the most public confession.

People can do many things as individuals without any compromise of conviction. In the Ancient Church, in the Apostolic Church, after Pentecost, Peter and the other Apostles, as well as the congregation, apparently still went to the Temple. They had prayer fellowship there. They went through all sorts of rituals, even with priests who did not confess Jesus as Messiah. It was a very peculiar situation until the Temple was destroyed in AD 70. But one thing they never did. They never invited unbaptized people from the Temple to participate in the mystery of receiving the Lord's body and blood. The writer of the Hebrews says, *"We have an altar from which those who serve the tent* (tabernacle) *have no right to eat".* So we shouldn't think of church fellowship in individual terms — this nice person, or that nice person. In fact, we can't see or determine who are Christians. We haven't that x- ray vision. Only God knows who are his people. When we talk about church fellowship, we are not talking about individuals, we are talking about finding the public marks of the Church, the voice of the Shepherd, the pure Gospel and Sacrament, where this is publicly functioning. When I hear pure preaching, Baptism and the Eucharist, there I know God is gathering his Church, but I cannot tell which individual actually has spiritual life. Only God can make that judgment.

So all of us deal with the Church by faith, not by sight. This Is Luther's great evangelical insight. This is quite the opposite from the way in which the contemporary ecumenical movement deals with the Church. Today the typical attitude to the Church is that we must see it. We have a great hankering to see this thing and not just leave it to faith.

Not The Way To Truth

What happens is that people tend to begin with the outward organization. When asked, What is Christianity?, they answer: Well, there is this big group of Christians here, and this group there, and there are hundreds of groups over here — put them all together under one roof and that will be the Church. The Archbishop of Canterbury, Archbishop Temple, one of the founders of the modern ecumenical movement, said, "I believe in one holy, catholic Church, and I deeply regret that it does not yet exist". He meant that the Church would be one catholic Church only when all these different groups were visibly in one organization, under one roof. Although he was too profound a man to have meant that, the rigidly logical consequence would be that this one Church is to be brought about by our efforts at ecclesiastical diplomacy, by a kind of churchly

Kissingerism, where you bargain — you give up this, and we give up that; I'll trade your Apostolic succession for the Real Presence, and so on. Everybody gives up something, and finally you come to some formula. This is not the way to Christian truth. What results is really walking by sight rather than by faith. You assume that, when you've gathered all these big statistical numbers, all these millions under one roof, this is the Church. Then you ask, Well, what does this conglomerate teach? And the answer becomes very vague. What do all these people agree on? Sometimes, very little. It's all quite topsy-turvy. Luther, on the other hand, does not walk by sight, but by faith. He teaches us to ask first of all, "Where can I hear the voice of the Shepherd?" Luther says: The Christian message is the known — the Church is the unknown.

A Compromise Liturgy

In 1817 the Prussian king determined to bring together the Lutheran and the Reformed Churches in his country. He had no evil intentions. He was a very devout man. The Prussian royal house had just experienced a terrible humiliation at the hands of Napoleon. Napoleon had overrun the whole of Prussia and gone all the way to Russia. He was finally beaten back by the great Russian General whose name is Winter. Winter has won Russia's wars for centuries. Nothing will move in the Russian Winter. Napoleon found that out. Miraculously, the Prussian and other European countries were suddenly delivered from the thraldom of Napoleon. The humiliation was over. There was a great resurgence of national feeling.

There was also a return to seriousness with regard to matters of faith. Now the king, with quite honorable intentions, thought just as many modern people think. The challenge of unbelief is so great today. We cannot afford to go on divided roads. Let's put all our efforts together and confront the common enemy. What he wanted to achieve was a union between the 90 percent Lutherans in his country and the 10 percent Reformed. The Prussian ruling house was Reformed. So he devised a common liturgy. He fancied himself somewhat of a liturgical scholar. He developed a liturgy on which he thought Lutherans and Reformed could agree. It's that liturgy that has the compromise formula which people could take the way they wanted to — quite an ingenious formula — a real piece of Kissingerism, where the form of distribution is, "Take, eat: Jesus says, this is my body ...". Do you see how clever that is? It doesn't confess what it is. It confesses what Jesus says it is, and then what he **meant** is completely open. A person who denies the Real Presence can say, "Yes, that's what he said, but, of course, he meant something else". And the Lutheran can understand what he means by it and everybody can be happy.

Pressure Exerted To Gain Acceptance

This classic union formula, "Take, eat; Jesus says, this is my body ...", leaves it wide open as to what it really is, because nobody has ever questioned that that is what he said. The only question is. What did he mean?

So, with this formula, the king thought he had solved the problem and everybody could unite. They had this service at the royal chapel, but not many followed the example. The Lutherans were certainly not inclined to accept it. At first, the king wanted this to be voluntary, but when these measures didn't work, the king decided to exert pressure. Really, for a modern country that prided itself on being progressive and modern, it was a terrible shame. The kind of thumbscrew tactics that the king used to compel his Lutheran subjects to accept the union, was an embarrassment throughout Europe. There were weird cases of pastors being persecuted like common criminals. The Lutheran liturgy, which was now forbidden, was celebrated at night in barns. One noble lady was fined 2000 ducats for allowing Lutheran services on her estate. Her carriage was confiscated as a fine.

The Lutheran Church of Australia

Out of this arose the great migration which led to the establishment of the Lutheran Church of Australia. For our Church in Australia, 1838 is an extremely important date, because the Lutherans under Pastor Kavel came here as a direct result of what had happened there, beginning with the 1817 forcible union of the Churches without real agreement in the doctrine of the faith. Both former branches of the Lutheran Church of Australia, which united in 1966, go back to this event. The Lutheran Church of Australia originated out of a deep confessional integrity, and a deep desire to preserve the faith which has been confessed by the Reformation fathers and laid down in the Book of Concord.

A Rich, Confessional Background

One of the things that Hitler did, was to try to combine the Lutheran and Reformed Churches for the sake of centralization and easier control. The Churches resisted. Imperial Bishop Mueller was appointed, but few obeyed him. A famous Church struggle ensued and, in the process, the Hitler administration was simply cast aside. Then in 1945 came the end. The sad thing was that the Churches, instead of using the new freedom that came with liberation, voluntarily did the very thing which Hitler had tried to force them into. As Dr. Sasse says, "In 1948, at the foot of the Wartburg, the Lutheran Church was buried". Dr. Sasse was then a professor at the University of Erlangen. He saw this happening. He understood, as few people did at the time, that, by this action, the Prussian union of 1817 was extended to the whole of Germany. Already an elderly man, Dr. Sasse left, and went to the uttermost parts of the earth — to Australia. What blessing his testimony here has been to all of us! He taught so clearly in matters of the Church, the Ministry and the Sacraments. Some of his writings on these topics will soon be available in English, translated by another Australian, Dr. Norman Nagel. Concordia Publishing House, St Louis, is about to publish them. From every point of view, the Lutheran Church of Australia has a rich, confessional background which should be a good foundation for meeting the sort of problems with which the devil, from time to time, is bound to assail us.

The Leuenberg Concord

In 1973 came what may well be regarded as the next logical development. All the Lutheran, Reformed, and Union Churches of Germany, which had united in administrative structure, but had pretended that they were not really in church fellowship, composed a document called the *Concord*. In that Concord they said that they now were in agreement, and that the division about the Sacrament no longer existed. Theirs had been a kind of *de facto* relationship. After the fact, the thing was sanctified by this document which is really a compromise. Our theologians strongly criticized it. Whole books have been written about it, pointing out that this is contrary to the confession of our Church. But the thing was accepted. The main push for it came from the Lutheran World Federation. A highly significant step was taken in 1977 by the Assembly of the Lutheran World Federation, accepting the ecumenical principle called "reconciled diversity".

No Longer Church Divisive

This means that there is to be complete church fellowship among the various Christian denominations, but all of them keep their confessions unchanged and regard each other as fully orthodox. In other words, this means that the Prussian union principle, where everybody keeps their confessions, but they no longer divide the Church, is now extended, not only to all of Germany, but since 1977, this principle is presented on a global basis. Action along these lines is being taken in America where, for example, some Lutheran Synods are now working toward full church fellowship with the Church of England, Methodist, Presbyterian, and so on. This would be a great blessing, and I would be the first to thank God if that were possible without compromise. But it is being done on the basis of "reconciled diversity", which means everybody may keep their doctrine and just forget the differences. That is not going to lead to any strong sense of conviction or to any real unity. It confirms the desperate confusion and flux which characterizes modern Christendom.

Division On The Sacrament

Marc Lienhard, one of the theologians of the Lutheran World Federation, has written a book, the English title of which would be: *Lutheran-Reformed Church Fellowship Today*. Here Lienhard explains how it could happen that after four hundred years of unsuccessful efforts to resolve the disagreements, a breakthrough came so quickly in our time. The basic reason was that both parties accepted a new attitude to Scripture. Both sets of theologians, the Reformed and the Lutherans, accepted the historical critical attitude to Scripture, that the Bible is not as such, or in any straightforward sense, the Word of God. That brought about the quick agreement. And then, in a sentence which really says a lot, he writes, "This new attitude to Scripture created new problems which were unknown in the 16th century. That became apparent at Arnoldshain when it was no longer possible to agree to connect the Institution of the Lord's Supper with the night in which Jesus was betrayed." What that means in simple, straightforward language is this: Many of the leading New Testament scholars in Germany, who participated in these discussions, did not believe, and therefore could not agree, that the historical Jesus Christ, who was crucified under Pontius Pilate, instituted the Lord's Supper.

In the article, *Jesus Christ*, by the leading New Testament scholar and a student of Bultmann, Hans Conzelmann, the author says that the historical Jesus never established a sacrament and had no idea of founding a Church. They claim that these things were not done by the historical Jesus. They were done after the Easter experience by the Early Church. In other words, the Christian communities invented it, under the impression of the figure of Jesus.

New Attitude to Scripture

To my mind, **the** great obstacle that we face world-wide, lies precisely in dealing with this new attitude to Scripture, which no longer acknowledges it to be without reservation, the Word of God. The trouble is, that we often find that it is being put like this: "Look, we agree. We agree that Jesus Christ died for us. Therefore, we are agreed in the Gospel. We agree in the Creed, so therefore, if we don't agree that the Bible is exactly the Word of God, that shouldn't divide us." I think it becomes clear how much of an illusion that is when you consider the article which one of the leading American Lutheran Bible scholars wrote. **Professor John Reumann**, a leading New Testament scholar in the Lutheran Church in America (LCA), wrote an essay for the 450th anniversary of the Augsburg Confession, which appeared in the June, 1980 issue of *Lutheran World Report*, the official organ of the Lutheran World Federation. The gist of the article is this: Article III (**Of the Son of God**) of the Augsburg Confession teaches basically the traditional dogma about Jesus Christ which had been confessed at Nicaea and Chalcedon. But the Bible does not really teach that, if one consults the Bible in the proper, that is, the historical-critical way. Therefore, the Reformation's *Scripture alone* principle should today prompt us to consider giving up Article III of the Augsburg Confession, in order to hold on to Article IV, **Of Justification**. The mind boggles. How **can** one hold on to justification, to any sort of Gospel of Christ, if one has to give up the confession that he is God?

World-Wide Dilemma

This represents the great dilemma that we face world-wide. This is why, world-wide, our churches need to find each other, work together patiently, not hysterically, under the Word of God and the Confessions of the Church, and stick to those things to which the Reformation has pointed us —the pure Gospel and the pure Sacraments, which illuminate and coordinate all elements of the faith.

I can well understand the magnetism, the attraction of friendly groups, particularly among our young people, when they find a group who are friendly, outgoing, radiant, smiling, positive, in a world that is cut-throat, cold and dreary. Perhaps, in their youthful enthusiasm, also some of their church life doesn't seem very satisfying. I just read a little slogan: "Cold churches, like cold butter, don't spread very well". When one finds groups that are warm and outgoing, deeply Christian and pious, one can understand the magnetism that this exerts. But then we need to see very clearly, that finally what builds the Church is not good feeling and friendliness — important as these things are, as an obligation on our part. What we need is only the Word and Sacrament of Christ, and for that, we should be prepared to put up with quite a lot of nonsense, too. Think of that poor Syrophoenicean woman, who came crying after the Lord in that desperate condition when her daughter was tormented by a demon. She came to the last man on earth who could help her, and she was apparently treated so shabbily. The Lord didn't even seem to care. He put her off several times. He said it isn't right to take the food of the children and give it to the dogs. If she had been a modern crusader for human rights, she would have said, "What, you call me a dog? I'll have you up for violation of my civil rights." The Lord makes her wrestle with him, and she becomes strong through that. In the end, he grants her wish. But how she had to put up with the coldness and seeming indifference from the Lord and from the group that surrounded him! The disciples said, "Send her away. Do something quickly. She's an embarrassment."

Many people would say today, "If that's the kind of people with whom Jesus associated, we don't want him. We'll seek help somewhere else." But when we have the pure Word and Sacraments, we must not be put off by human frailty and human weakness that we see on every hand and, above all, in ourselves. The Church is not to be seen. She is not an article of sight. "**I believe** one holy Christian Church." We do not say, "I **feel** one holy Christian Church".

Chesterton said, "Of all the false religions in the world, the worst is the worship of the God within — enthusiasm". That Jones worships the God within, turns out ultimately to mean that Jones worships Jones. What a prophetic use of a name, when you think of Jonestown, Guiana, where tragedy happened some 40-50 years later. The true tragedy of Jonestown is not the poisoned Kool Aid. It's the spiritual poison which is repeated much less dramatically elsewhere.

The Lutheran, July 30, 1984
Christian News, November 19, 1984

1. What article of faith illuminates all the others? ____
2. What is the essence of church fellowship? ____
3. In 1817 the Prussian King determined to ____.
4. What led to the establishment of the Lutheran Church of Australia? ____
5. Sasse said that in 1984 at the foot of the Wartburg the ____ was buried.
6. What is significant about the Leuenberg Concord? ____
7. What attitude toward the Bible brought about agreement? ____
8. Many leading New Testament scholars in Germany could not agree that historical Christ instituted ____.

9. What did Hans Conzelmann say? ____
10. John Reumann, an LCA scholar taught that the Bible does not really teach ____.
11. The Church is not an article of ____.
12. The true tragedy of Jonestown is not the poisoned Kool Aid but ____.

WHAT DOES BAPTISM MEAN FOR DAILY LIVING?

January 7, 1985

How many of you have read *The Living Bible*? If you look at the translation of the sacramental texts, you will find there that figures of speech are repeatedly introduced. Everything is made into a symbol, where the New Testament text speaks literally. This translation does it to Baptism as well as to Communion. But the New Testament does not regard Baptism as a sign or symbol, or as a reminder of somehow having entered the life of God in some other way. This is the very place where it happens! This is the objective place where God bids us grab hold of him and trust him.

Complete In The Cross
The cross is not merely to be received and then ignored. The cross is to be borne. It is not an accident that at the time of a Baptism, the celebrant says to the baby: "Receive the sign of the holy cross, both upon the forehead and upon the breast, in token that you have been redeemed by Christ the crucified". It is Baptism that takes one into the cross. The ancient Christian sign of the cross is also appropriate in connection with the formula, *"In the name of the Father and of the Son and of the Holy Spirit"*. That was an ancient Christian custom, long before the Papacy arose. In this simple gesture, it symbolizes that the Trinitarian faith is the faith which trusts God in the cross. Everything has happened in the cross and is complete there.

In answer to the question in his Catechism — *"What benefits does God give in Baptism?"*, Luther says: "In Baptism God forgives sin, delivers from death and the devil, and gives everlasting salvation to all who believe what he has promised".

And to the question — *"What does Baptism mean for daily living?"*, Luther answers: "It means that our sinful self, with all its evil deeds and desires, should be drowned through daily repentance; and that day after day a new self should arise to live with God in righteousness and purity forever".

Our Crosses Blessed By Christ's Cross
This is an extraordinarily important thing, that the new life in Baptism is actually lived. Jesus says: *"If any man would come after me, let him deny himself and take up his cross"*. In Baptism, we receive the high privilege to bear the cross, and to know that the crosses, which God gives us to bear, have first been blessed by his cross. If his cross had not blessed our crosses, they would prove a curse, and they would be unbearable. But when Jesus blesses our cross by his cross, then it is holy, then it is blessed; then nothing but good for us and our loved ones can come from it.

Daily Drowning Of The Old Adam

One of the most impressive sermons I have ever heard was preached by an old retired pastor in Germany. I was passing through Hamburg and he was preaching on this very thing: Baptism and the renewal this means, and the daily drowning of the Old Adam. He was holding forth with great gusto about how important it is to drown the Old Adam. We do that, he said, by repentance. This great evil reality in us is drowned. Then he stopped and said. "But the blighter can swim. He comes up again every day, so you have to deal with him all over again every day." This is why the Lord says that he who follows him is **daily** to take up his cross.

Crucifying The Flesh

We should be very suspicious of those fresh-out-of-camp Christians who say that they have no more problems because they had this beautiful experience with Jesus and all is well. They are not afraid. They have suddenly eclipsed St Paul and in a few hours have become more sanctified and more holy than the great Apostle, who complained in Romans 7 of the great civil war that bothered him all the time. For him there was a constant struggle unto death between the flesh and the spirit. Is it very likely that one of us will advance beyond St Paul, and whereas he had that struggle, shall be relieved of it? I don't think that is very likely. But it is a great comfort to be realistic about it, to know that there is nothing abnormal about it. It is the normal lot of Christians **daily** to bear the cross, and **daily** to have to fight down the flesh, not just to trim it down a bit and reform it, but to crucify it — and that hurts! That's not easy.

What Is Spirit Baptism?

Now I come to another matter which has become very controversial and has bothered many people. How are we to think of the idea of a Spirit Baptism? People say to us: "It's all very nice that you have been baptized; but that's not the real thing. That's only water Baptism. The real thing that you should strive for, besides water Baptism, is Spirit Baptism. Then you really have something."

There is some slight variation in definition, but largely Spirit Baptism is defined as an experience which is usually signaled by speaking in tongues or something like that — some miraculous works. We need to see very clearly that the New Testament does not talk about two Baptisms, the New Testament quite clearly speaks only of one Baptism. In fact, it rubs it in (Ephesians 4:5), *"There is one Lord, one faith, one Baptism"*. Only one Baptism! This one Baptism is not a water Baptism, and it is not a Spirit Baptism. It is a *water and Spirit Baptism together*. It's a sacramental Baptism, and you can't tear these two apart. As Paul says in Ephesians, water and Word washing go together.

Two Classes of Christians?

It's a fundamentally mistaken idea to think that there are two types of Christians in the Church: there is the normal crowd who have only water Baptism, and then there are the special elite, who have also had

Spirit Baptism. How awful that is! It creates two classes of Christians. There is a sort of first class and an economy class — those who have the Spirit in this way, and those who don't have the Spirit. St. Paul, and all the writers of the New Testament, make it quite clear that Baptism places us all into one body, one temple. There are no class distinctions. Whatever race or nationality or social background we come from — in Jesus Christ all are one. There is only one kind of baptized Christian. We need to remember that, too, when strife and distress trouble Christian congregations, and divisions happen and people are annoyed with each other, and fly off into different directions.

I am reminded how important this is through a joke that comes from Czechoslovakia at the time of the Soviet suppression of the Czechoslovak freedom fighters. Do you remember how Dubcek, Prime Minister in 1968, tried for a few weeks to maintain what he called "socialism with a human face"? The thing was put down by Soviet tanks and the whole experiment went down in flames. After the Soviet invasion of Czechoslovakia, some journalist asked Dubcek: "Do you regard your Soviet invaders as brothers or as friends?" Without a moment's hesitation he replied, "As brothers, of course, because you can choose your friends!"

"All One In Christ"

That is how we have to regard ourselves in the Church. We are baptized into the one Church. We haven't chosen one another on the basis of pleasant personalities who appeal to one another. We are not common interest group with the same temperament and the same inclinations, who flock to each other like birds of a feather. We are completely different sorts of people from all walks of life, sometimes quite incompatible, temperamental and difficult, and all this sort of thing. Yet we are all baptized brothers and sisters. We don't choose one another. We are put together. We are born as brothers and sisters from our great Heavenly Father, with our Church our common mother. Therefore, Baptism commits us to sticking together, through thick and thin, no matter what. We are the Church of God, baptized brothers and sisters under the one Father.

To make this point about Spirit Baptism a little more concrete, let me quickly take you on that four stop guided tour of the *Book of Acts*, which our charismatic friends usually conduct at this point. If you talk about this with one of these Spirit Baptism people, they will give you these great examples from the *Book of Acts*. Whenever people came to Christ in faith, the normal thing was that at a later stage, or possibly even at the same time, a second thing happened, namely, a visible Baptism of the Holy Spirit. They remind you that at Pentecost men suddenly started speaking in many languages. In Acts 8 we have the record of Philip at work in Samaria. Many believed and were converted. Then a second thing happened some days later. They were visibly baptized with the Holy Spirit. The same thing happened — Acts 10 — to Cornelius and his friends. They were baptized and spoke in tongues. In Acts 19, we have the interesting case of John's Baptism. Why this guided tour?

"Into All The World"

Imagine a sight which you meet in any Australian pub: a bulls-eye in the middle and several concentric circles around the outside, and you throw your darts. Now the Lord's mission program can be presented like this: central bulls-eye, represented by Jerusalem and Judea. Jesus said, Wait in Jerusalem and then take this message from Judea to Samaria, the next circle, and then to the uttermost parts of the earth. So the mission of the Church was not a completely unsystematic, chaotic running in all directions. The Church was to be thoroughly founded and grounded in Jerusalem, from there to the adjoining territory of Samaria, closely related to the Jews, and then to the Gentiles — into all the world.

A Kind of Mini-Pentecost

The business of special Spirit manifestations, special tongues or miracles, things like that, do not just happen. They are reported — especially this special Spirit gift — at these crucial places when the Gospel crosses one of these boundaries. That's when kind of mini-Pentecost occurs. It happens precisely when the next phase of missionary work is introduced, in Acts 8 — Samaria — there is a kind of mini-Pentecost, if I might say that without irreverence. Then the next boundary is crossed to the Gentiles —Cornelius —and again there is a kind of repetition of Pentecost as languages are given. Finally, there is the special case of Acts 19 among those who had only John's Baptism. What does all this mean?

The special manifestation of the Spirit occurs just at those places and nowhere else. It emphasizes precisely the point that I was making before about the unity of the Church. There are no first and second classes in the Church. Whether you are a Samaritan Christian or a Gentile Christian, you are not on a lower rung than the most rigorously practicing Christian in Judea or in Jerusalem itself.

The Church of Jesus Christ Is One

You may say why go to all the bother to make that point? If we look at the history in the *Book of Acts*, it is quite clear why that is necessary. The Jews had been so imbued with the idea of their superiority and that everybody else wasn't even worth touching, that they would travel around Samaria, the long way, just to avoid setting foot in that unholy place. They hated these people. Even Peter, when called to go to the Gentiles, had his doubts whether he should go. And so he was given that vision of the "heavenly ham" coming down. Peter is told to cut and eat. No! Peter is cleaner than God. He doesn't want to touch this filthy thing. God has to tell him, "Don't call unclean what I have made and called clean." It is a very hard, lesson for Peter to learn — very hard to be deprogrammed from this idea that Jews are superior to everybody else. Lest there be any temptation to superiority, God himself, the Holy Spirit, by action, manifests that Samaritan Christians and Gentile Christians are just the same as the original Jerusalem congregation. The Church of Jesus Christ is one and has the same dignity everywhere. That's the real meaning of this manifestation.

Just a few little details! In Samaria you have this wretched magician, Simon, trying to buy the gift of giving the visible manifestation of the Spirit. He saw that this was given through the laying on of the Apostles' hands. Note, it didn't happen through every Tom, Dick and Harry. It happened only through the laying on of the Apostles' hands. Even Philip, the evangelist, couldn't do it. He converted these people, but only when the Apostles came personally, was a special manifestation revealed.

There is an interesting text in 2 Corinthians 12:12, where St Paul says that all the signs of an Apostle were done among the Corinthians, and he mentions miracles, powers, and so on. Clearly, the *Book of Acts* and the New Testament mean to present this whole miraculous aura, these special healings, tongues and prophecies, as a kind of glow that surrounds the divine institution of the Apostles and Prophets.

Foundation and Superstructure

After the Apostles were gone, these gifts did not continue. And I believe there is good theological reason for that. Consider Ephesians 2:20, where Paul says, *"You are built upon the foundation of the Apostles and Prophets, Christ Jesus himself being the cornerstone, in whom the whole structure is joined together and grows into an holy temple in the Lord". Notice, "the foundation of the Apostles and Prophets"*. There is a qualitative distinction —foundation is foundation, and house is house. You don't keep building the foundation. You build the house on it. The foundation is laid down once and for all, and then you go on from there.

It is wrong for us simply to assume that the same thing that applied to Peter and Paul applies also to us. They were Apostles. They were a part of the foundation of the Church. We are not. We are the building. The theological intention of the *Book of Acts* is quite clearly to attach this special aura of miracle to the divine institution of the Apostolate at the founding of the Church. From then on, the Church grows on that divinely-provided foundation.

So you have in Apostolically-founded congregations like Corinth special miraculous manifestations. But there is no reason to believe that every Tom, Dick and Harry had all these gifts. Otherwise these texts don't make any sense.

I come now to the interesting and exceptional case in Ephesus recorded in Acts 19. This again takes place in the Gentile world. These people are asked, "in whose name have you been baptized?" Into the name of Jesus." "Did you receive the Holy Spirit when you were baptized?" "No, we have never even heard that there is a Holy Spirit."

The "Release" of the Spirit

Now, that is not possible. Every Jew knew Psalm 51, *"Take not thy Holy Spirit from me"*. They were not illiterate. Having been baptized by John, they must have known something of the Old Testament. It is not possible to think that they simply didn't know, or hadn't heard anything about, the Holy Spirit. You have an exact parallel in John 7, where it says literally, *"The Spirit had not been given, because Jesus was not yet glorified"*. Of course, the Holy Spirit was God from eternity, but the Spirit hadn't been ***"given"*** yet, hadn't been ***released*** yet. Acts 19 is an absolutely parallel construction. *"We have never even heard that the Holy Spirit has been given."* (NIV)

That is the only way you can make any sense out of it, because look what Paul does then! Supposing they had said, "We have never even heard that there is a Holy Spirit". If that were the meaning, then Paul should have given them a sermon about the Holy Spirit. He does nothing of the kind. He tells them about Jesus. He tells them about the work of Jesus, who has, by his work, released the Holy Spirit. So they knew about the Holy Spirit. What they didn't know was that the work of Christ, the divine Savior, had been accomplished. Therefore, all this that they had been waiting for had now been completed.

After they hear about Jesus, then they are baptized. It is quite clear that they had received the Baptism of John. Some people take offence at that and say, if they really had the Baptism of John, why are they baptized again? They try to find reasons in the text to say that they had a kind of misunderstood Baptism of John. But there is nothing in the text to suggest that it wasn't a genuine, valid Baptism.

John's Baptism Was Provisional

What about the thousands who were baptized on Pentecost? Wouldn't you think that most of them had already been baptized by John? I am convinced of it. All Jerusalem, all Judea — all came to John. All the pious people had been baptized by John. It seems very hard to assume that all these good people who became founding members of the Jerusalem Church, still hadn't gone to John. The most obvious assumption is that most of them had already been baptized by John. Now they receive Christian Baptism. The real meaning of the Acts 19 text is that John's Baptism, together with the whole figure of John, is provisional.

Provisional Replaced With Permanent

You have to be careful with that. That is not saying that it did not convey forgiveness. It was a Baptism of repentance, but forgiveness is also attributed to it. Even the Old Testament sacraments provided forgiveness in a different mode or manner. What we need to see is that John the Baptist is this unique *provisional forerunner* whose ministry is limited to one thing. His Baptism is limited to this preparatory stage. The final, permanent thing, is what is launched at Pentecost. This strange passage in Acts 19 means to signal that Christian Baptism is more than just provisional impartation; it gives a completeness which did not exist before the cross and the resurrection. This is something which happened only as a result of the cross. The provisional now needs to be replaced with the permanent.

Our Lord himself tells us about John the Baptist. He says this when people come to ask about him: *"Among those born of woman there has risen no one greater than John the Baptist; yet he who is least in the kingdom of heaven is greater than he"*.

> He who stands in the fullness of the New Testament has a status greater than that provisional ministry that John the Baptist exercised, which was in the nature of the shadow, on the verge of being converted into the reality itself.
>
> THE LUTHERAN, (Australia)
> Christian News, January 7, 1985

1. The Living Bible makes everything into a ____ where the New Testament text speaks ____.
2. What does God do in baptism? ____
3. He who follows Jesus is ____ take up his cross.
4. Spirit Baptism is usually defined as ____.
5. The New Testament talks of only ____ baptism.
6. There are no ____ classes in the church.
7. Most of the thousands baptized at Pentecost were already baptized by ____.

REGULAR PRAYER AND THE MINISTRY

October 7, 1985

Let the word of Christ dwell in you richly, as you teach and admonish one another in all wisdom, and as you sing psalms and hymns and spiritual songs with thankfulness in your hearts to God. **Colossians 3:16**

"I will not let Thee go except Thou bless me!" — Gen. 32:26

"Train yourself for piety. For physical training has some limited value — but piety is of boundless value!" — I Tim. 4:7.8

(J.B. Phillips: "Take time and trouble to keep yourself spiritually fit. Bodily fitness has a certain value, but spiritual fitness is essential.")

I. Daily Prayer

The church's worship is governed by an annual ("Christ-half" and "Church-half") rhythm, and a weekly rhythm (AC and Apol. XXIV). But there is also a daily rhythm: "Give us this day our daily bread. . ."

Contrary to popular impression, the apostolic church's worship was not messily "spontaneous," or chaotic. Acts 2:42 ("the prayers") seems to suggest set, liturgical prayers. Where did these come from?

The Jews at the time of the Lord's earthly life followed a well-established pattern of piety in stated prayers at stated times throughout the day (see K.F. Mueller and W. Blankenburg, Leiturgia, v. III, pp. 100-294: "Der taegliche Gottesdienst." Cf. A. Schmemann, Introduction to Liturgical Theology). There were prayers said at the time of the morning sacrifice in the Temple, in the afternoon, and at the time of the evening sacrifice. There were also set prayers for mealtimes and at bed-time. Certain psalms were long associated with these particular times, e.g. Ps. 63 for morning prayers, Ps. 141 ("and the lifting up of my hands as the evening sacrifice") for the evening, and Ps. 4 at night.

The apostolic church continued to observe the customary hours of prayer, no doubt with New Testament adaptations (see Acts 2:15; 3:1; 10:9; 12:12). Besides "psalms" there were also "hymns" (perhaps the OT canticles) and "spiritual odes" (Col. 3:16). The latter were not camp-fire "songs" but theologically rich, Spirit-filled hymns like the New Testament canticles in Lk. 1 and 2, and perhaps also creedal statements like Phil. 2:5 ff. or I Tim. 3:16.

Luther's concrete suggestions, in the Small Cathechism, to heads of households and schoolmasters, about the daily prayers for morning, evening, and meal-times, to be taught their families or pupils, are completely in this spirit.

II. Ministers and Prayer

The whole priestly People of God are engaged in daily prayer — but His ministers especially so: "But we will give ourselves continually to prayer, and to the ministry of the Word" (Acts 6:4). To impart "doctrine" without prayer is arid intellectualism or cold professionalism; to practice "prayer" without doctrine is fetid mysticism.

Luther to Ministers:
"Now that they are free from the useless, bothersome babbling of the Seven Hours, it would be fine if every morning, noon, and evening they would read, instead, at least a page or two from the Catechism, the Prayer Book, the New Testament, or something else from the Bible and would pray the Lord's Prayer for themselves and their parishioners. In this way they might show honor and gratitude to the Gospel, through which they have been delivered from so many burdens and troubles, and they might feel a little shame, because, like pigs and dogs, they remember no more of the Gospel than this rotten, pernicious, shameful, carnal liberty" (*Large Catechism*, Preface).

To replace various medieval prayer-books with evangelical material, Luther published the *Prayer Book* in 1522 (*Luther's Works*, vol. 43, pp. 11-45). This, as well as *A Simple Way To Pray*, for his friend Peter, the Master Barber (LW, 40, 189-211), consists largely of guides for meditating and praying through the basic parts of the Catechism, viz., the Commandments, the Creed, and the Our Father . (H. Sasse: "Our Confessions can be prayed. The Book of Concord should be for the Lutheran pastor what the Breviary is to the Roman Catholic priest"). In meditating on various texts Luther fashions "a garland of four strands." First, instruction. "Second, I turn it into a thanksgiving; third, a confession; and fourth, a prayer" (p. 200).

All this, however, presupposes a churchly context, with daily Matins and Vespers, at least in villages big enough to have schools (*Luther's Works*, 53,12,13). Today, when daily prayers as a rule no longer take place in Lutheran churches, at least the ministers of the church might find in these ancient churchly forms a fitting frame for then own prayers. Seminaries are appropriate places to install life-long devotional patterns, to equip the servant of the Lord for his spiritual battles, and to render him as independent as possible of his own moods or "ups and downs": "And although these daily services might not be attended by the whole congregation, the priests and pupils, and especially those who, one hopes, will become good preachers and pastors, should be present" (*Luther's Works*, V. 53, p. 13).

Luther's own spiritual and theological life was deeply steeped in the Psalms, which are sturdier fare than sugary modern "devotional" literature. In antiquity the entire Psalter was recited once a week. Note also the beautiful daily rhythm of promise/fulfilment, as expressed by the progress from the Martins canticle (the Benedictus) to the Vespers canticle (the Magnificat)!

Ora Et Labora!

III. Resources

H. Bitzer, *Light on the Path* (Baker, 1982). Daily Greek and Hebrew reading with helps.

H. Lindemann, *The Daily Office* (CPH, 1965).

George Kraus, *By Word and Prayer* (CPH, 1977).

On Psalms:

The Interlineary Hebrew and English Psalter (Zondervan, 1970).

Ronald Knox, *The Book of Psalms in Latin and English* (Sheed and Ward, 1948).

K. Marquart
Pentecost, 1983

P.S. See C.S. Lewis, Letters To Malcolm, Chiefly on Prayer.

Ed. This article was sent to us by Paul T. McCain of Defiance, Ohio, who wrote: "I've enjoyed your recent two articles on the spiritual life of the clergy. I thought you might like this. Professor Kurt Marquart passed it out to a class I recently had with him at Concordia Theological Seminary." We know that Professor Marquart practiced what he preaches in this article already thirty years ago when we were roommates at Concordia Seminary in St. Louis. It is of utmost importance that seminary professors impress upon seminarians the need for the regular prayer life. Surveys show that many pastors admit that their own personal prayer and devotional life is rather shallow. The charismatic movement is not the answer to this problem. Those who want more articles on this subject should read Professor Marquart's articles on worship, liturgy and the seven sins in *The Christian News Encyclopedia*.

Christian News, October 7, 1985

1. ____ fitness is essential?
2. The whole priestly People of God are engaged in ____.
3. To impart doctrine without prayer is ____.
4. Luther's own spiritual and theological life was deeply steeped in the ____.

PROFESSOR MARQUART DISCUSSES LITURGY FROM CONFESSIONAL VIEWPOINT

June 6, 1988

Q: Could you give us a proper theological basis for liturgy/liturgical worship?

R: Within the given space limits only a few rough observations are possible. "Liturgy" is not primarily form, and therefore taste and "culture" have little to do with it. It is first of all content, and means public service or duties in general, and the Service of Word and Sacrament in particular (AP XXIV, 79-81). This liturgy "is preserved among us in its proper use, the use which was formerly observed in the church, and which can be proved by St. Paul's statement in I Corinthians 11:20 ff., and by many statements of the Fathers" (AC XXIV, 35). If with the New Testament one believes in real means of grace as central and crucial (I John 5:7-8), then one will understand worship "in spirit and in truth" (John 4:24) incarnationally and sacramentally — and that necessarily means "liturgically." If on the other hand one does not accept the centrality of the means of grace, then that text becomes a pretext for man-centered sentimentality, emotionalism, psychobabble, etc., in short, "spiritualizing."

Q: What is adiaphora and what isn't, in the worship/liturgy?

R: Since there is no Levitical law in the New Testament, almost anything is an "adiaphoron" —except, I suppose, the Words of Institution and the Lord's Prayer. But, of course, "adiaphoron" does not mean that one may do whatever he likes. Sunday, the whole church year and the basic structure of the Service are all "adiaphora." But they are not therefore to be sacrificed — least of all, in favor of cheap secular vulgarities borrowed from TV mindlessness. When we know ourselves to be humble pilgrims and followers of the glorious company of the apostles, the goodly fellowship of the prophets and the noble army of martyrs (**Te Deum**), then we shall want in our worship to express identification, solidarity and continuity with the true Church of all times and places (I Cor. 14:36).

The liturgy, moreover, is the bearer of the church's confession. As the custodians of these treasures, the public ministry must guard them against vandalism. It is sad when "official" organs of the church themselves act as the vandals. Our forefathers well understood that adiaphora are no longer adiaphora when confessional implications are involved (FC X). C.F.W. Walther, in his *Pastoral Theology*, recognized that whether something is a "confessional ceremony" depends on the historical situation. He listed the non-breaking of the sacramental bread, the use of the Apostles' Creed and the renunciation of the devil at Baptism among the ceremonies which had in his day to be maintained against Calvinism (p. 56). One could not give them up, said Walther, "without weakening the confession of the pure doctrine." What would he have said about the Fundamentalist/ Pentecostal furies which are now devastating our liturgical life?

The founding fathers of the Missouri Synod were deeply devoted to Christian liberty and abhorred all legalism, from bitter experience. In this genuinely evangelical spirit they wrote into their synodical constitution:

Furthermore, Synod deems it necessary for the purification of the Lutheran Church in America, that the emptiness and the poverty in the externals of the service be opposed, which, having been introduced here by the false spirit of the Reformed, is now rampant.

All pastors and congregations that wish to be recognized as orthodox by Synod are prohibited from adopting or retaining any ceremony which might weaken the confession of the truth or condone or strengthen a heresy, especially if heretics insist upon the continuation or the abolition of such ceremonies. The desired uniformity in the ceremonies is to be brought about especially by the adoption of sound Lutheran agendas (church books) . . .

Synod as a whole is to supervise how each individual pastor cares for the souls in his charge. Synod, therefore, has the right to inquiry and judgment. Especially is Synod to investigate whether its pastors have permitted themselves to be misled into applying the so-called "New Measures" which have become prevalent here, or whether they care for their souls according to the sound Scriptural manner of the orthodox Church (*Concordia Historical Institute Quarterly*, VOL XIX, no. 3 (Oct. 1946), pp. 12-13).

From the Cornerstone, Concordia Seminary, Ft. Wayne
Christian News, June 6, 1988

1. What is the bearer of the church's confession? ____
2. The fathers of the Missouri Synod deplored all ____.

LITURGY AND EVANGELISM

March 21, 1994

"The true secret and significance of evangelistically attractive worship lies beyond the reach of a shallow, psychologizing and trivializing pragmatism. This part of the chapter will attempt to suggest some parameters relevant to Lutherans in modern America" (58).

"It is this concrete Word-and-Sacrament liturgy that, according to the Augsburg Confession, 'is preserved among us in its proper use, the use which was formerly observed in the church and which can be proved by St. Paul's statement in I Cor. 11:20 ff. and by many statements of the Fathers. The church, in this view, meets in solemn public assembly not to conduct pep rallies for worthy causes, or to boost a religious talk with publicity stunts, but to transact the awesome and life-giving 'mysteries of God' (1 Cor. 4:1). God and his gifts are all-decisive, not man and his moods" (59-60).

"Two comments will round out the picture. First, it must never be forgotten that good preaching, that is 'practical and clear sermons,' constitutes the church's strongest missionary attraction. This major element of the liturgy is the minister's most demanding task. He may not escape from it—for instance by exchanging the role of shepherd, who feeds and defends the flock, for that of sheep dog, harassing sheep brigades to 'do the real work' themselves.

"The second point is about the Holy Supper. Since it is rude even in ordinary life to receive gifts without saying thank you, it goes without saying that God's great gifts are to be received with thanksgiving. Therefore, in this secondary sense, 'the ceremony [of the Lord's Supper] becomes a sacrifice of praise.' Its primary and basic nature and purpose, however, is that of pure gift or Gospel: Forgiveness, life, and salvation are freely granted to penitent sinners in the very body and blood of the Lamb, by which these gifts were won. More is the pity that much 'liturgical' fashion today again turns the sacrament into a sacrifice, contrary to Luther's great evangelical breakthrough. Impressive ceremonial edifices can then be erected on such faulty foundations, but the more such structures gain in cultic, symbolic weight of their own, the more they can do without the real New Testament Holy of Holies, the really present body and blood of the God-Man. The sacramental presence may or may not he affirmed in such schemes—it is simply no longer central or crucial. By way of contrast, the vital meaning of the Sacrament as pure gift (1 Cor. 10:16-17) is confessed in Krauth's splendid pronouncement: 'The Sacramental Presence is the necessary sequel, the crowning glory of the Incarnation and Atonement. . . . The glory and mystery of the Incarnation combine there as they combine nowhere else.'

"**Liturgy,** then, is much more than forms and ceremonies, which are in themselves indifferent. It is first and foremost a firm theological content, namely, the holy Gospel and sacraments of God. Taken in this nontrivial sense, liturgy cannot be in competition with evangelism. After all, the 'Spirit, the Water, and the blood' of the liturgy are the very agents ('witnesses') of World evangelization! 'Make disciples of all nations' and 'This do in remembrance of me' go hand in hand. Ultimately, of course, the worship of God is its own end, while evangelism is a means to that end. The highest worship of God on earth is faith itself— 'and the Catholic faith is this, that we worship one God in three persons and three persons in one God' (Athanasian Creed). There will come in time, however, when the complete will replace the incomplete, and the caterpillar of faith will turn into the glorious butterfly of beatific sight (1 Cor. 13:8-12). Death itself will then be swallowed up in victory (1 Cor. 15:54), and all mission work or evangelism will cease. But the New Jerusalem will make the new heavens and new earth resound forever with the worship of God, the Lamb, and the Spirit (Rev. 19-22)" (61-62).

"Connected with good order **is** the matter of the stability of liturgical form. There are two aspects to this stability. One is the principle of continuity with the ancient church. The church of the evangelical Reformation wishes to be neither a newfangled sect nor a biblicistic one which imagines that it can bypass the whole intervening history of the church. Wanting to be simply a faithful continuation of the orthodox church of the ages, it makes a point of having 'introduced nothing, either in doctrine or in ceremonies, that is contrary to Holy Scripture or the universal Christian church'" (63-64).

"A certain healthy variety is of course built into the liturgy itself by way of the church year. So it **is** a wrong kind of variety, not variety itself, which ought to be criticized. In his 1523 *Formula Missae* (Form of the Mass) Luther, with characteristic bluntness, expressed his hesitancy about changing accustomed forms,

> and more so because of the fickle and fastidious spirits who rush in like unclean swine without faith or reason, and who delight only in novelty and tire of it as quickly, when it has worn off. Such people are a nuisance even in other affairs, but in spiritual matters, they are absolutely unbearable.

"In his German Mass of 1526 he deplored 'the great variety of new masses, for everyone makes his own order of service.' The implication is that not everyone can do it equally well. A certain variety in rites has always existed, said Luther, but 'it would be well if the service in every principality would he held in the same manner and if the order observed in a given city would also be followed by the surrounding towns and villages.' 'As far as possible we should observe the same rites and ceremonies, just as all Christians have the same baptism and the same sacrament [of the altar] and no one has received a special one of his own from God'" (65).

From Lutheran Worship - History and Practice
Christian News, March 21, 1994

1. What constitutes the church's strongest missionary attraction? ____
2. The highest worship of God on earth is ____.
3. The church of the evangelical Reformation introduces nothing that is contrary to ____.
4. Luther said that it would be well if the service in every principality be ____.

GOLD, SILVER, AND BRONZE AND CLOSED COMMUNION

June 1, 1998

The famous Olympic prize medals often serve as handy historical markers. One might say, for instance, that the 16th century, culminating in the Book of Concord, was the Lutheran Reformation's golden age. The 17th century would then represent its silver age. After that comes bronze-which then inspires various efforts to return to former glories. Applying this to the Missouri Synod, the time of Walther might be taken as its golden age, and Pieper's as the silver age. The "bronze age" would then describe more mediocre times, marked partly by complacent self-satisfaction, partly by zeal for inherited clichés the full meaning of which is no longer grasped, and partly by rebellion against the perceived mindlessness or callousness of the "tradition."

A typical Bronze Age trait is the idea that whatever I personally am accustomed to is "what has always been done." For example: "Pastor, why can't we sing good old hymns like 'The Old Rugged Cross' instead of these newfangled ones like 'We All Believe in One True God'?" One can sympathize with the perception and the sentiment, but one should be under no illusions about what is really old and what is new here.

Or take the matter of Closed communion. First of all, is it "close" or "closed"? Actually, "close" is simply an older form of "closed" as in "close carriage." So, despite the touching stories that have been made up about "close" communion and why that is so much better than the "exclusive," and therefore politically incorrect "closed" communion-the fact is that "close communion" and "closed communion" mean exactly the same thing. The opposite of both is "open communion," not something like "distant communion"!

But which is the original practice and which the deviation, open or closed communion? There can be no doubt that during Missouri's "golden" and "silver" ages, that is, under Walther's and Pieper's leadership, closed communion was the single standard, drawn from Scripture and Confession. There was a clean break between confession and denial, truth and error, church and sect. Then, with the sudden switch to English after World War I, came the onslaught of the ways of "American Evangelical Protestantism." One prominent feature of this was the pervasive sense of the various "denominations" as friendly rivals, their differences "man-made." This is how Billy Graham put it in his 1953 book: *Peace with God*:

> The New Testament teaches that while there is actually only one church there can be any number of local churches formed into various denominations and societies or councils. These local churches and denominational groups may be divided along national and theological lines, or according to the temperament of their members ... I am always tempted to point out how many different styles of hats have come to be designed for both American men and women. We all belong to

the same human race, but we all have enough physical differences to make it impossible for us to wear the same style of hat with equal satisfaction (pp. 175, 177).

A sea-change in the Missouri Synod came with the "Statement of the Forty-Four" in 1945-belatedly now endorsed by a former president of the Missouri Synod.[1] The inner logic here led to a collapse of orthodox and heterodox churches as viable categories in the practice of fellowship. After all, if only a congregation, but not "the synodical organization," is really "church," then the whole notion of a confessional church, as all Lutheran fathers including Walther and Pieper knew it, dissolves into a rickety patchwork of "man-made" regulations, puffed up perhaps as contracts or "covenants of love" freely entered into, and the like. What came now to the fore instead of the category of churches was the notion of individuals (i.e. "Christians who differ from us" or "Christians of different denominations," etc.). And why should man-made "denominations" get in the way of "fellowship" with "other Christians"?

This Bronze Age confusion of tongues naturally drained much of the conviction out of Close Communion. That practice came to be seen by many as a quaint Synodical "policy" on a level perhaps with the old Roman Catholic regulation against eating meat on Fridays!

All this lies behind the recent Florida-Georgia polemic against "a denominational or synodical requirement" on would-be communicants at our altars (*Celebrate!* Pentecost 1996). Substitute "confessional" for "denominational or synodical," and the case is perfectly clear: "Neither Scriptures nor the Confessions impose a confessional requirement on baptized Christians who desire to confess the Real Presence and receive the body and blood of Christ offered in the Eucharist." The sentence is clearly false in light of just Acts 2:42 and Rom. 16:17 for starters, not to mention Gal. 1:8-9 and all other texts which forbid complicity with false teachings and with those who support them.

Unlike that weasel-word "denomination," the word "confession" is very biblical indeed, St. Mt. 10:32, and it embraces the entire life-giving truth the Lord has entrusted to His church, St. John 8:31-32. Does it include the central truth about justification by grace alone? Or the truth that baptism actually works regeneration? Or that the Lord gives His very body and blood under bread and wine, and not just "spiritually by faith," but bodily, and into the mouth of every communicant, regardless of faith? To deny that issues like these irreducibly define the Gospel is to reject the whole Bible as understood in the Lutheran Confessions. Yet, it is just such issues over which the various "denominations" traditionally differ, not to mention the modern horrors of casting to the winds any Word of God, which inconveniences anybody!

Are members of other "denominations," who regularly (or irregularly!) attend the sacramental rites of their own (officially heterodox) churches, to be willy-nilly admitted also to the altars of the orthodox church, simply on their own say-so? If yes, as *Celebrate!* argues, then it is profoundly untrue that "Lutheran Christians do not disagree in their doctrinal understanding of the Lord's Supper. The primary areas of disagreement concern practice, about those who are to be welcomed as guests when a congregation celebrates the Eucharist" (*Celebrate!* Lent 1998). There is something very wrong with any "doctrinal understanding of the Lord's Supper" which can so cavalierly tear that holy Sacrament loose from its natural setting in the fullness of the "apostles' doctrine" (Acts 2:42), and from what that means for church, Gospel, confession, ministry, and fellowship.

The Lent 1998 *Celebrate!* which has just been sent to us, and I assume to all Missouri Synod pastors, presents itself as a "Bible Study." It is in fact a very slanted piece of advocacy, which claims to cover the Words of Institution and the "only passages in the remainder of the New Testament that deal with the Eucharist," but never mentions Acts 2:42 or the clearly Eucharistic Rom. 16:17 (see the "kiss of peace" in V. 16)!

One can fully sympathize with the plight of ministers of certain ages, who had been trained in the warm and fuzzy ways flowing from the "Statement of the Forty-Four," and who feel like fish out of water as the Synod tries to reclaim its older, sounder confessional heritage. They were wronged by those who misled them. But with all the human sympathy in the world we dare not lose sight of what really is biblical and confessional and what is not; what is old and what is new; what is standard and what is eccentric. The best book on the subject is still Werner Elert's *Eucharist and Church Fellowship in the First Four Centuries*. Here's a sample: "Since a man cannot at the same time hold two differing confessions, he cannot communicate in two churches of differing confessions. If anyone does this nevertheless, he denies his own confession or has none at all" (p. 182).

[1]Ralph A. Bohlmann, Missouri Lutheranism, 1945 and 1995, *Lutheran Forum*, vol. 30, no. 1 (February, 1996), pp. 12-17.

Christian News, June 1, 1998

1. "Close" communion and "closed communion" mean exactly ____.
2. A sea-change came in the Missouri Synod with ____.
3. Which former president of the LCMS endorsed "the Statement of the Forty-Four?"____
4. The Bronze Age confusion of tongues drained much of the conviction out of ____.
5. The word "confession" unlike "denomination" is very ____.
6. What does the Florida-Georgia publication Celebrate promote? ____
7. What did Werner Elert say about communing in two churches of differing confessions? ____

"LUTHERAN WORSHIP AND THE GOLDEN MIDDLE

May 17, 2004

"We need desperately to find our way back to that golden middle way of the Holy Scriptures and or Reformation heritage, which is in fact the historic and official position of our Synod." (p. 10)

The May 2004 Lutheran Witness *published statements from each one of the five candidates for the presidency of the LCMS. The statements are reproduced on page 8. Did Dr. Kurt Marquart "shoot himself in the foot when he promoted the "golden middle" and expressed concern about "a clericalist elitism in the spirit of J.A.A. Grabau and Wilhelm Loehe" in the LCMS? Did he lose the support of those who distributed buttons at a Concordia Seminary, Fort Wayne, Indiana, symposia which referred to themselves as "hyper-euros" following in part Loehe and Grabau, churchmen who took issue with C.F.W. Walther's defense of the rights of laymen and congregations?*

It is true that some referred to as organized conservatives prefer a candidate who is not as outspoken against a growing sacerdotalism in the LCMS as Marquart. However, Marquart's "golden middle" position is precisely why a growing number of Missourians who consider themselves "right in the center" of where the LCMS has always stood are being attracted to Marquart.

Dr. Marquart began his statement in the *Lutheran Witness:*

I. The single most crucial issue facing our Synod, in my view, is the progressive loss of spiritual, doctrinal unity. There is, for instance, the acceptance of evolution by some within the Concordia University System, and there is the neo-Pentecostalism of "Renewal in Missouri." There is much confusion on the nature of the Gospel ministry. At one extreme there is the temporary "licensing" of ill-trained persons for "Word and Sacrament ministry," contrary to Augsburg Confession XIV. At the other, there is a clericalist elitism in the spirit of J. A. A. Grabau and Wilhelm Loehe, who opposed first LCMS President C.F.W. Walther's position that the Gospel-preaching ministry is indeed a divine institution, but is "owned" by and accountable to Christ's church or congregation. Interestingly enough, Loehe himself admitted that Walther's position on church and ministry was exactly that of the great Reformer, Martin Luther! We desperately need to find our way back to that golden middle way of the Holy Scriptures and our Reformation heritage, which is in fact the historic and official position of our Synod. A great obstacle to the honest facing of issues is the new doctrine put forward by the Commission on Constitutional Matters, in connection with the David Benke/Yankee Stadium case, that prior approval by one's "ecclesiastical supervisor," exempts one from disciplinary action on Biblical and Confessional grounds. This is an intolerable return to pre-Reformation thinking. Our Confessions insist that no one may "allow the authority of any person to count for more than the Word" (Treatise on the Power and Primacy of the Pope"). Christians have the right and duty to appeal to the Word of God in all matters of dispute, and this right may not be squelched bureaucratically (see Gal. 2:11-21).

No other candidates for the presidency has spoken out as boldly against neo-Pentecostalism in the LCMS and the acceptance of evolution in the Concordia University System as Dr. Marquart. Most LCMS officials, including LCMS President Kieschnick, prefer to push the growing evolution controversy under the rug. Crisis In Christendom—Seminex Ablaze shows that nothing is being done about evolutionists on the LCMS's clergy roster. Marquart's criticism of "a clericalist elitism in *the* spirit of J. A. A. Grabau and Wilhelm Loehe" does not mean that he is opposed to sound liturgy and worship or that he is promoter of the modern Church Growth movement.

His book opposing the Church Growth Movement, a movement which LCMS President Kieschnick with his *Ablaze* program enthusiastically supports, was commended by an LCMS convention.

When it comes to liturgical matters and worship Marquart has ever since his student days advocated "the Golden Middle." *A Christian Handbook on Vital Issues*, an 860 page book which *CN* sent to all delegates to the LCMS's 1973 convention, includes several articles by Dr. Marquart in which he promotes the golden middle. Unlike some theologians, he is not constantly shifting from one extreme to the other. "Some Aspects of a Healthy Church Life" is one of the Marquart articles in *A Christian Handbook on Vital Issues*. This essay originally appeared in the *Lutheran Synod Quarterly*, Mankato, Minnesota, reprinted in the *Lutheran Theological Journal*, Adelaide, South Australia and then in the August 18, 1969 *Christian News*.

Dr. Marquart wrote in this essay.

Less obvious is the status of the Sacrament. Here many observers believe that the Real Presence, while strenuously defended in, has in recent times not played the central practical role in church life which it had in apostolic, ancient, and Reformation times. This means, however, that the corrective is not something new to be obtained from the modern Liturgical Movement, but something old already given in Biblical, Lutheran theology.

Despite valid insights, the Liturgical Movement is dangerous because of its Romanizing sacramentalism, sacerdotalism, and just plain externalistic ritualism. The view of the Sacrament as something essentially sacrificial, something that we do toward God, rather than vice versa, is fundamentally wrong (Heb. 10). The Office of the Ministry is thought of as some kind of new Levitical priesthood, into which men are admitted not by the call of the congregation, but by the laying on of hands in ordination. This leads to a theory of "Apostolic Succession" in one form or another, since the Ministry in this view can be conferred only by one who is already a member of this self-perpetuating order. It is surprising that Romanizing Lutherans can ardently embrace such ideas, when they are rejected in the clearest possible terms in the *Treatise of the Power and Primacy of the Pope,* especially paragraphs 60-72! To deny the conflict is sophistry.

Dr. Marquart is a contributor to *Lutheran Worship-History and Practice,* a 640 page book published by Concordia Publishing House and authorized by the LCMS's Worship Commission. *Christian News* has sold many copies of this book. It is still available from *Christian News.* "Lutheran Worship Is Christocentric," the lead story in the March 21, 1994 *Christian News* quoted at considerable length from Marquart's contribution to this book. *CN's* report and editorial on the book follow. Here again Marquart takes the Golden Middle position. He has not changed. Those who want to make ordination something of a sacrament and who support Loehe and Grabau's put down of the laity and congregations are the ones who have changed in their overreaction to the Church Growthers.

Lutheran Worship - History and Practice
Christian News, May 17, 2004

1. Marquart opposed a growing ____ in the Lutheran Church-Missouri Synod.
2. The single most important issue facing the LCMS is ____.
3. What is being accepted in the Concordia University System? ____
4. Loehe and Graubau opposed ____.
5. Loehe admitted that Walther's position on church and ministry was exactly that of ____.
6. Should prior approval by one's "ecclesiastical supervisor" exempt one from disciplinary action? ____.
7. Nothing is being done about ____ on the LCMS clergy roster.
8. Despite valid insights the Liturgical Movement is dangerous because ____.
9. The Office of the Ministry is thought of as ____.
10. Who is ardently embracing "Apostolic Succession?" ____

CONTEMPORARY SERVICES

December 23, 1974

Sir:

May I join the fray re "contemporary services"? Let me throw in ten points, not as finished absolutes, but as challenges to serious discussion. To serve clarity and brevity, they are stated rather baldly and provocatively. But they are not meant to attack or offend anyone, least of all my young friends. They are intended to help beat off from the ecclesiastical tent the snout of that insolent contemporary camel, the Youth Cult! And that was created not of course by youth, but by bankrupt adults. Our Christian youth must not be sacrificed to this ugly Moloch.

1. The traditional Liturgy ought to be kept up to date, for example by eliminating "thou's" and possibly other stilted RSV-isms. (*Jerusalem Bible* is good!)
2. The Liturgy grows through the centuries like a beautiful coral reef, by way of gradual addition and modification. It is not a "program" which could be instantly concocted from scratch.
3. All the variety needed is provided by the changes throughout the Church Year. Immigration Sunday, National Eucalyptus Tree Week, Mothers' Day, Youth Sunday, and the like, tend not to liturgical enrichment but to maudlin humbug.
4. The Liturgy offers plenty of scope for "embroidering" upon the standard framework, especially by way of chants and hymns (of the latter in particular we could use a lot of good new stuff). But it will not do to replace standard parts, like the Creed, the Our Father, the Sanctus, with pious gabble regarded as "contemporary".
5. To be an effective vehicle of devotion, the Liturgy requires loving familiarity and disciplined practice. An itch for constant change and novelty makes for a shallow, immature, unstable devotional life. It confuses worship with entertainment.
6. The Liturgy is God-centered, Christ centered, Word-and-Sacrament centered, heavenly, objective, corporate. Many attempts to be "contemporary" end up merely giving vent to man-centered whims, exhibitionism, wordy vulgarity, and unbridled subjectivism. The Liturgy celebrates newness of life, and must not cater to the old Adam's fleshly and worldly hang-ups and conformities. The music must draw to heaven — not reek coarsely of Saturday night's raucous fertility-rites!
7. The Liturgy expresses the devotion of the whole people of God, from baptized infant to aged saint. It is degrading to the Church and harmful to youth to ape the secular isolation and adulation of youth on a pedestal by itself. In any case, a healthy society imparts its values to its young. A culture, which simply crawls to the whims of "youth", is sick and contemptible. Indulgent doting and fawning are selfish and destructive forms of love.

8. Christians of all ages are to be taught to respect the Church as their mother, and to learn from her millennia of experience. Genuine liturgical development is based on knowing, loving adaptation of inherited treasures. Whatever our age, we are all only young upstarts in relation to our mother, the Church. Hence, we must beware of the spoilt-brat attitude, which knows everything better, and is prepared to chop and change with little or no understanding of the Church's accumulated wisdom.
9. Solzhenitsyn still vividly remembers the holy and heavenly impact which the Russian Liturgy made on him as a small child, an impression which "no personal suffering and no intellectual theories were able later to erase". Children who have been properly led into an appreciative participation in the Liturgy will find razzmattazz substitutes repulsive!"*
10. In the Lutheran Church, Christian liberty and liturgical freedom do not mean that "anything goes". Article 24 of the Augsburg Confession and the Apology expresses firm principles about what the Liturgy is and ought to be.

* This observation rests scientifically on agreement by 100% of those 60% of my children old enough to express a significant opinion, 70% of my family being under 13!

The Lutheran, September 9, 1974,
Christian News, December 23, 1974

1. What tends to maudlin humbug? ____
2. An itch for constant change and novelty makes for ____.
3. Many attempts to be "contemporary" end up merely ____.
4. Children who have been properly led into an appreciative participation in the Liturgy will find ____.

INDEX

39 Articles – 12
Abendmahl – 43
Ablaze – 108
Absolution – 3,56
Adiaphora – 44,45
Adiaphoron – 99
Agnus Dei – 7
ALC – 64,67
Altar – 2
Anglican Articles – 12
Anti-sacrementalism – 12
Apostle's Creed – 4
Apostles – 93
Apostolic Doctrine – 16
Apostolic Succession – 109
Archbishop Temple – 82
Arians – 50
Arnoldshain – 85
Ascension – 58
Atonement – 70
Augsburg Confession – 45,66
Augustine – 27
Australia – 28,61
Baptism – 20,21,70,89
Beatitudes – 24
Beck, William – 21,22,23,27
Benke, David – 107
Bereavement – 60
Bible Class – 27
Bishop Preus – 67
Bonhoeffer, Dietrich – 15
Book of Acts – 92,93
Book of Concord – 104
Bronze Age – 105
Budget – 6
Bultmann, Rudolf – 86
Calvin – 76
Calvinism – 79
Calvinistic – 41
Calvinists – 61
Catechism – 78
Celebrate! – 105,106
Charismatic movement – 98
Chemnitz, Martin – 15,29,72
Christian Liberty – 22
Christianity – 82

Christmas – 4
Church – 23,60,87
Church attendance – 37
Church fellowship – 65,81
Church Growth Movement – 108
Church Growthers – 109
Church music - 49
Church politics – 67
Close Communion – 81,104,105
Communion – 27,34
Communion Liturgy – 61
Communion with Christ – 12,33
Communism – 10
Concord – 85
Concordia Seminary, Ft. Wayne – 100
Concordia University System – 107,108
Confession – 105
Consecration – 61,62
Conservative Reformation – 31
Contemporary services – 110
Conzelmann, Hans – 86
Council of Nicaea – 4
Council of Trent – 67
CPH (Concordia Publishing House) – ii,12
Creation – 20
Cresset - 15
Cross – 55
CTCR (Commission on Theology and Church Relations) – 66
Cullmann, Oscar – 41,58
Czechoslovakia – 91
Decision card – 55
Denomination – 105
Devil – 54
Dimension – 59
Disney, Walt – 45
Distribution – 61
Dix, Gregory – 61
Dogma – 8
Dubcek – 91
Dudko, Dimitri – 47
Early Christian Worship - 58
Easter – 58,59

Eckhardt's REALLEXICON – 34,43
Ecumenical Movement – 10,66,82
Elert, Werner – 106
English – 104
Entertainment – 47
Enthusiasm – 87
Epiphany – 10
Epistle – 4
Eucharist – 6,29,41,76,82
Eucharistic – 72
Evangelism – 46,101,102
Every Sunday – 32
Evolution – 107,108
Faithful Word – 26
Fellowship – 73
Fields, W. J. – 12
Fish – 58
Forgiveness of sins – 57
Formula Missae – 102
Formula of Concord – 29,66
Funerals – 71
Galbraith, Kenneth – 37
Galesburg Rule – 65
Gehrke, R. – 15
Geneva – 18
Gerhard, John – 15,30,34,42
Gloria in Excelsis – 4,45
Golden Middle – 107
Gospel – 18,24,46,70
Grabau, J. A. A. – 107
Gradual – 4
Graham, Billy – 38,104
Hamann, Henry P. – 66
Heaven – 59
Historical-critical – 85
Historical-criticism – 68
Hitler, Adolph – 84
Holland – 60
Holy Communion – 32
Holy Spirit – 94
Holy Supper – 101
How Great Thou Art – 38
Hyper-euros – 107
Invocation – 3
Irenaeus – 29
Isaiah Mighty Seer – 49
Jesus – 60

Joad, C.E.M. – 66
John's Baptism – 94
Jonestown – 87
Joy – 59
Jungkuntz, R. – 15
Justification – 81,86
Justification by faith – 31,69
Koinonia – 73
Krauth, Charles Porterfield – 31,40,65
Kyrie – 3,45
Law and Gospel – 24,71
Lent – 12
Leuenberg Agreement – 79
Leuenberg Concord – 85
Lewis, C.S. – 37,39,44,47
Liberalism – 15
Lienhard, Marc – 85
Liturgical Movement – 12,108
Liturgical Substance – 37
Liturgy – 1,2,7,8,28,47,48,60,99,101
Liturgy/liturgical Movement - 99
Lochner, F. – 13,15,43
Loehe, Wilhelm – 107
Lord's Day – 58
Lord's Supper – 31,41,70
Luther, Dr. Martin – 5,33, 26,28,52,56,107
Lutheran Church – 18
Lutheran Church of Australia – 84
Lutheran Churches of America – 81
Lutheran Hour – 38
Lutheran Observer – 13
Lutheran Service – 35
Lutheran Witness – 107
Lutheran World Federation – 10,67,68,85
Lutheran World Report – 86
Lutheran Worship-History and Practice – 109
Lutheraner – 13
Magna Carta – 21
Mass – 32,33
McAfee, J. B. – 13
McCain, Paul T. – 98
Meaningful Worship – 1

Means of Grace – 18,19,41
Melanchthon – 81
Meuser, Fred W. – 65
Meyer, Scott – ii
Minneapolis Theses – 64
Missouri Synod – 10,37,44,66
My Faith Looks Up To Thee – 49
Nagel, Dr. Norman – 84
Napoleon – 83
Narthex – 2
Neary, Roy – 39
Neo-Pentecostalism – 107
New English Bible – 27
New Lutheran Church – 78
New Testament – 28
Newman – 12
Nicene – 4
Nuremberg – 42
Ohlendorf, Ray – i
Old Adam – 90
Open communion – 104
Ordination – 109
Ordination – 12,109
Otten, Herman – iii
Our Way of Worship – 33
Paradise – 9
Pentecost – 91,94
Pentecostalism – 108
Phillips, J.B. – 40
Pieper, Francis – 20
Preaching – 47,101
Preaching House – 26
Preus, David – 64
Private Communion – 34,81
Propers – 3
Propitiatory – 72,76
Prussian King – 83
Psalms – 97
Purgatory - 69
Real Presence – 60,78
Reception – 61
Rechthaberei – 74
Reconciled diversity – 85
Redemption – 20
Reed, L. – 15,33
Renewal in Missouri – 107
Resurrection – 58
Reumann, Professor John – 86

Revised Standard Version – 27
Revivalism – 2
Roman-Lutheran dialogue – 67,69
Rome – 10,18
RSV-isms – 110
Russian Liturgy – 111
Russian Orthodox – 46
Sacerdotalism – 19,107,108
Sacerdotalist – 12
Sacrament – 6,14,28,49,56,70,108
Sacramental – 4,71
Sacramentalism – 19,108
Sacrifice – 72
Sacrificial – 4,71
Sanctification – 20
Sanctus – 7
Sasse, Dr. Hermann – 32,43,58, 73,75,81,84,97
Scripture – 86
Scriver – 15
Scriver, Christian – 15,31
Secret religious societies – 65
Sermon – 2,5
Sermon and sacrament – 43
Services – 60
Shakespeare – 7
Solzhenitsyn, A. – 60,111
Soviet Union – 47
Speaking in tongues – 90
Spielberg, Steven – 39
Spirit – 93
Spirit Baptism – 90,91
Spiritists – 59
St. Ambrose of Milan – 50
St. Augustine – 6,50,60
St. John Chrysostom – 62
Statement of the Forty-four – 105
Stephen – 59
Symbol – 89
Syncretism – 64
Synodical Conference – 10
Te Deum – 99
Testament – 74
Thanksgiving – 70
The Living Bible – 89
The Lutheran Hymnal – 37
The Lutheran Liturgy – 15,33
The Lutheran Standard – 64

Theology of Fellowship – 66
Theology of Glory – 67
Theology of the Cross – 52
This Is My Body – 75
Tongues – 91
Traditional Liturgy – 110
Transubstantiation – 60
UFO – 39
Unionism – 64
United Testimony of Faith and Life – 64
Vatican II – 60
Walther, C.F.W. – iii,21,24,30,32, 34,44, 99,104,107
White, Larry – ii
Wittenberg "Concord" – 75
World Council of Churches – 10
Worship – 1
Wurmbrand, Richard – 39
Yankee Stadium – 107
Youth – 28
Youth Cult – 48,110
Zwingli – 74
Zwingliism – 61